THE ULTIMATE GUIDE TO THE
RIDER WAITE TAROT

ABOUT THIS BOOK

"It is possible to interpret Tarot cards reliably when one focuses on their images and symbols. Hard and fast interpretation schemes are not always suitable for this purpose—in fact, in many cases they even make it more difficult to access the symbolism that is really there, for symbols are many-faceted and open to various interpretations; it is easy to get lost in a jungle of different possibilities. The present book provides a welcome aid in such situations. For each of the 78 Tarot cards a concise description of the ten most important of the depicted symbols and their essential aspects is given." *(kup-Pressedienst)*

"The book is like an amazing toolbox (or sewing box). At last, one understands all the symbols and is well able to interpret the cards for oneself." *(Pia Schneider)*

The authors' long years of experience make sure that this book represents a reliable source of advice and a practical aid with a wealth of experts' tips.

THE ULTIMATE GUIDE TO THE
RIDER WAITE TAROT

JOHANNES FIEBIG &
EVELIN BÜRGER

FIRST AMERICAN EDITION
Thirteenth Printing, 2020

Cover design by Lisa Novak
Editing: Claudia Lingnau-Lazar, Constanze Steinfeldt, and Connie Hill
Images on the cover and in contents are from the Rider Waite Tarot, copyright held by US Games Systems, Inc., Stamford CT USA. Further reproduction prohibited. Rider-Waite is a registered trademark of U.S. Games Systems, Inc.
Translated from the German language original by Charles Warcup
Typesetting, lithography: Stefan Hose, Goetheby-Holm, and Antje Betken, Oldenbuttel / Germany

Original German Edition, Krummwisch, near Kiel, 2008

Copyright © 2008 by Koenigsfurt-Urania Verlag GmbH
D-24796 Krummwisch, www.koenigsfurt-urania.com

Llewellyn Publications is a registered trademark of Llewellyn Worldwide Ltd.

Library of Congress Cataloging-in-Publication Data
Fiebig, Johannes.
[Tarot-Deutung—leicht gemacht. English]
The ultimate guide to the Rider Waite Tarot/Johannes Fiebig & Evelin Burger ; edited by Barbara Moore.—First American Edition.
     pages cm
ISBN 978-0-7387-3579-5
1. Tarot. I. Title.
BF1879.T2F5413 2013
133.3'2424--dc23

Llewellyn Publications
A Division of Llewellyn Worldwide Ltd.
2143 Wooddale Drive
Woodbury, MN 55125-2989
www.llewellyn.com

Printed in the United States of America

ACKNOWLEDGMENTS

Our thanks go to those who have participated in our seminars and whose experience and observations have made a valuable contribution to the wealth of symbolic interpretation to be found in this book. And we would like to thank all those colleagues from whom we have been privileged to learn so much: Margarete Petersen, Luisa Francia, Rachel Pollack, Marion Guekos-Hollenstein, Judith Bärtschi, Hajo Banzhaf, Gerd B. Ziegler, Eckhard Graf, Jim Wanless, Klausbernd Vollmar and especially Lilo Schwarz, whose trailblazing book *Im Dialog mit den Bildern des Tarot*. The English edition, *In Dialogue with the Imagery of Tarot* 2005, has earned an excellent reputation through its lucid treatment of the details contained in the Rider/Waite Tarot—E.B / J.F

Contents

An Overview of the 78 Cards

Swords

Pentacles

10 reasons for writing this book

People have often asked us to do so.

We would like to gather together the knowledge and insights which we have gained in the course of a quarter of a century in our work as tarot authors and in conducting seminars (not only for the benefit of our readers, but also for ourselves).

We like to write about tarot!

Life is too short to waste time with substandard interpretations.

The Rider / Waite cards contain a wealth of things still waiting to be discovered—by ourselves and by our readers (so we are hoping to receive your feedback!).

At present the main focus of our work is on publishing, so we do not have as much time as we would like for giving lectures and seminars. This book can go some way towards filling the gap.

Many people have problems with some of the tarot cards. We would like to encourage readers to look a little more closely at the contents so as to be able to draw their own conclusions.

And we hope that this will help sharpen readers' perception for their everyday lives, so that they are better able to look beyond what seems like a straightforwardly good or bad incident or experience and perhaps discover a deeper significance.

We have never written a book such as this before. It struck us as being a helpful —and interesting—idea to summarize the essentials briefly and concisely.

One can occupy oneself with a subject such as the tarot for 25 years without it becoming boring. (On the contrary, getting older is the prerequisite for accessing certain kinds of knowledge.) We would like to share these aspects, too.

Evelin Burger & Johannes Fiebig

Tarot interpretation—the easy way

The 10 best Tarot definitions

"The true Tarot is symbolism; it speaks no other language and offers no other signs." (Arthur E. Waite)

"Tarot is one of many possible stairways into your depths." (Luisa Francia)

"The tarot addresses one's intuition from a stance which lies between the intellect's cold rationality and the realms of mystical fancy." (*Die Zeit*)

"The tarot could be described as God's Picture Book, or it could be likened to a celestial game of chess, the Trumps being the pieces to be moved according to the law of their own order over a checkered board of the four elements." (Lady Frieda Harris)

"Tarot is spiritual poker." (Mario Montano, alias Swami Prembodhi)

"Tarot is the yoga of the West." (Robert Wang, as well as Hans-Dieter Leuenberger)

"Tarot is a good servant, but a bad master." (Hajo Banzhaf)

"Tarot works, because the messages in the images have an effect on your consciousness which simultaneously influences your lived reality as well as acknowledging the existence of a higher Will and entering into a state of harmony with it." (Gerd B. Ziegler)

"Tarot is the ideal bridge-builder: At the point where you seem to be able to go no further, you can build a bridge by dealing a spread of cards. The symbols on the cards show you new paths. You try them out. And then new possibilities become apparent in real life as well."

(Johannes Fiebig)

"The Old World may take pride in the fact that with the Tarot it has produced its own esoteric system—a school for training emotional intelligence, the wisdom of the heart and that of the soul which has neither been devised by priests or pharaohs, nor by cabbalistic scribes, but has been engendered through the collective subconscious of the Occident." (Eckhard Graf)

The 10 most important facts about Tarot

1 The tarot is a card deck containing **78 cards** according to a given system: the 22 cards of the 'Major Arcana' and 56 cards of the 'Minor Arcana' (arcana [singular arcanum] = secrets, mysteries). The Minor Arcana is subdivided into four suits: the Wands (or Staves), the Cups, the Swords and the Pentacles (or Coins).

2 The cards of the tarot were developed in **Milan and Bologna** during the Italian Renaissance around 1430. The identity of the first artist to paint tarot cards is obscure; all we know is that Bonifatio Bembo, whose name is occasionally mentioned, was not the first. Playing cards had already been in existence for at least 800 years before the first tarot cards were designed.

3 The tarot deck was the first one for which trump cards were defined. The tarot cards were used for centuries as a parlor game without any significance beyond **a simple game of cards.**

4 Only as late as the nineteenth century (to be exact in 1781) do we find evidence indicating that tarot cards were used for **esoteric interpretation** through their symbolism. The nineteenth century saw a great upsurge of interest in classical occultism. Many small groups devoted themselves to the study of tarot symbolism, often independently of each other. During this period cards of any kind were used to foretell the future.

5 The present worldwide expansion of tarot interpretation began in the western world during the **1970s.**

6 Since then, **new standards** have become so well established that we now tend to accept them as a matter of course. They include the huge variety of different tarot decks. Today there are over one thousand different versions, of which **many hundreds are currently available** on the market.

7 **The large number of ways of using the tarot** and creating spreads also represents a relatively recent phenomenon that we now take for granted. At one end of the spectrum we have large spreads that are used on certain significant dates or on occasions that are important to the individual user, and at the other end there is the solitary card for the day.

8 The **card for the day** is drawn either in the morning or in the evening, generally without the user formulating a particular question. The single image provides information, both in respect of the present situation and the task in hand, as well as an impulse for the next step.

9 Knowledge of the **four elements Fire, Water, Air, and Earth,** together with their association with the four suits Wands, Cups, Swords, and Pentacles, represents a key feature of modern tarot interpretation. Anybody can acquire the information involved (see pages 18–19 and 73) and then start on his or her own journey of interpretation.

10 Practically everywhere these days, the cards are seen as **mirrors.** This represents a completely new development, unknown during the Renaissance and in the nineteenth century. In their capacity as mirrors, the tarot cards always provide an opportunity for self-reflection. And: one cannot look into the mirror *for* others (*with* others, yes).

10 favorite ways of using a SINGLE card

1 **The card for the day.** This card represents a daily guide. It may point out an opportunity, a task, or simply some aspect that needs attention. You can see it as your daily guardian angel or companion.

2 **The card for the week.** This card highlights the topic of the week. It is as if you take a magnifying glass to concentrate on, for instance, a particular station of the tarot or a certain type of symbolism or theme during the space of a week.

3 **The card for the month.** This provides an outline of the situation, task, and next steps to take for a given month. You turn your attention to a single tarot card and study it with special care and awareness. And you develop with it!

4 **The year card.** This card represents the main theme running through your whole year. You can draw it on your birthday, at the new year or on any other defined occasion. Usually, the year card takes on a range of different aspects and provides different impulses as the year progresses. This is what

Suggestions for use:

- Think about the question(s) which you wish to address with the help of tarot. Take your time, and make sure that you are sitting or standing comfortably, but alert. Try to breathe freely. Now just listen—not outwardly, but inside yourself.

- Then you will find the central question forming within you. Take it up, refine it and express it to yourself as clearly as you can!

- However, when you pick a card for a day, a month or any other period of time, you can dispense with the specific question and simply ask: "What does the tarot want to say to me today/for the coming month/etc.?"

- Now shuffle all 78 cards together.

- Make sure the images remain face downward so that you cannot see them.

- Now draw the card (or cards for spreads) in the way that is customary for you and try to do this in a state of relaxed concentration.

- Place the card face down in front of you, or multiple cards in the order and pattern of the given spread.

- Now turn the single card over or the cards of a spread one by one.

- The card or the spread provide the tarot's answer to your question.

makes it so interesting, for it greatly clarifies your various personal affairs and questions.

5 **The project card.** The significance of the card is to be interpreted in the same way as in the cases already dealt with, only here it is to be related not to a particular week, year, etc., but to the duration of a specific project.

6 **The favorite card.** This card is not to be drawn, but consciously selected. Which card do you like best? Which card is your favorite at this moment?

7 **The personality card.** Work out the sum of the digits of your birth date (e.g. 3rd September 1968 = 9 / 3 / 1968, which yields 9 + 3 + 1 + 9 + 6 + 8 = 36. If the sum lies between 1 and 21, then the Major Card of the deck which has the same number is the respective personality card. (The *Major Cards* are the ones with both a number *and* a subtitle.) For instance, if the sum is 19, then the respective personality card is the one with the numeral XIX - *The Sun*.

If the sum is 22, then the personality card is the 22nd Major Card, i.e. *The Fool* with the figure 0.

However, if the sum is 23 or higher, as in the example above, then you have to work out the sum of the digits of the original sum. In the example, the digits of 36 would be added to make 3 + 6 = 9. The Major Card with the equivalent numeral is then the personality card, in this case IX - *The Hermit*.

8 **The essence card.** When the sum of the digits of your birth date is a number greater than 9, then one can sum the digits of that number to find the 'essence card'. Example: the personality card is number 14, and the summed digits of this number produce 5, so the card with the numeral V - *The Hierophant* is the essence card or core card. When the number of the personality card is less than 10, then the personality card and the essence card are identical. Then you can work backwards and find out the other card in the Major Arcana which has the same digit sum. Example: the personality card is *VII - The Chariot*. In that case *VII - The Chariot* is also the essence card. And *XVI - The Tower* can be used as your personal supplement because it has the same digit sum of 7.

Generally, the essence card need not be taken quite as seriously as the personality card, which remains, as it were, the decisive factor, because it describes something which is specific to the corresponding date of birth. The essence card and the supplementary card with the same digit sum are to be regarded simply as 'add-on' cards for the personality card.

9 **The complementary card.** Many interpreters see the *Fool* not only as the card at the beginning of the tarot, but also as the 22nd Major Card, in other words as *the* card which stands for the Whole and the ultimate Fulfillment. In most cases, there is a card which represents the *difference* between your personality card and the *Fool*. (Example: if your personality card is the 14, then the difference between it and the *Fool* is 22 − 14 = 8, i.e. the Major Card No. VIII is your *complementary card*. This is the card which marks the rest of the way, the unconscious which remains to be illuminated in order to 'complete' one's own personality.

10 **The digit sum or quintessence.** Using the same method as with the personality card (see No. 7), one can add the digits of all the cards of a given spread.

To do this, count the court cards (Queen, Knight etc.) as well as the *Fool* as zero and aces as 1. Using the sum, follow the same procedure as described for the personality card. The Major Card corresponding to the sum calculated is known as the *digit sum card* or *quintessence*.

The meaning behind the quintessence is this: the spread is and remains complete as it is; i.e. the quintessence does not produce anything new. But it represents a summary of the spread, something like a headline. Or it may function rather in the same way as a checksum is used to check the integrity of data.

The 10 most important rules for interpretation

1 The cards are mirrors.

The cards are like the 'mirror, mirror, on the wall': they help us to see and understand ourselves better. But of course they do not in themselves carry a guarantee that their user will always draw the correct conclusions. If you stand in front of your mirror at home and always say: "I'm the greatest, most beautiful etc.,"—or "I'm the stupidest, most ugly of all etc.," well, the worst-case scenario is that you will be right all the time! In that case you needn't expect the mirror to start talking to you and correct your rather one-sided opinion of yourself.

But tarot cards are a set of tried and tested tools that can help us to *become aware* of misleading, arbitrary beliefs. You will find the instructions for using them below. There are many ways of expanding our perspectives with the tarot, and when we apply these new insights in our everyday lives, we find new solutions appearing as if from nowhere.

2 Every card has positive and negative meanings.

This is the most important rule to bear in mind in order to be able to grasp the full scope of the symbolism. The authors have never met anyone who was able to see all 78 images spontaneously, without any external help, in both a positive and negative light at one and the same time—and they themselves were unable to do it without the benefit of training either. This facility only comes after a longish period of gathering experience with the tarot and with oneself.

3 Concentrate your energies on hard and fast reference points.

Some cards tend to give our imagination too much rein. For instance, we may be afraid that the Fool is about to fall over a cliff. In fact, there is no real evidence in the image to support this idea. Who knows whether the Fool will go on forward, turn back, or indeed whether the cliff is in fact a cliff—perhaps it is nothing more than a little outcrop. The card does not provide this information and so there is no point in dwelling on it.

An interpretation is plausible when it is coherent and makes definite sense to the observer—so long as this personal evaluation is based on actual clues to be found in the image.

4 **Differentiate between subject level and object level as the need arises.**

These terms were coined by the Swiss psychologist C. G. Jung for the purposes of interpreting dreams. On the object level, the figures and scenes in a dream (or here depicted on a tarot card) stand for other people and external events. Seen from the point of view of the subject level, the same figures and scenes become mirror images, facets of one's own personality and inner affairs.

An argument or conflict in a dream or on a tarot card may serve to work through—or indeed to prepare for—an actual controversy involving people who really exist. But the same dream or the same tarot card can, under different circumstances, also be indicative of an inner struggle.

The question as to whether the subject level or the object level provides the right perspective in any given situation needs to be answered on a case by case basis. If in doubt, you can consider both possibilities.

5 **Learn to recognize and take account of associations.**

The past two hundred years have witnessed the development of a broad literature of interpretation for the tarot. A number of general standards have become established, first and foremost with respect to the assignment of the four suits to the four elements. Thus the cards of the Cups suit stand for the element water, which in turn is associated with the soul and the psyche and all their various aspects.

The personal associations which occur to one may seem to involve quite unconnected things, e.g. in the case of the *Four of Cups:* "Wasn't that a lovely holiday last year!", "It's time to spend some time outdoors!", or "This figure with his crossed arms really irritates me—like my husband / child / colleague etc. when they refuse to listen to me ... "

Personal associations like this are certainly part of reading cards, and they make the process of interpretation more colorful and concrete. But: by placing too much emphasis on personal notions and associations in tarot interpretation we run the risk of chasing our own tails and simply reinforcing the thinking patterns which we already have. That is why it is important to get to know both levels of interpretation —personal associations *and* interpretation standards—and to be able to keep them apart.

Then we often find new perspectives emerging in everyday life. To keep to the example above, you may realize that you don't just need any kind of holiday, but it is high time for a period of reflection. Or the spouse/child/colleague etc. who seems to be as clammed up as the figure on the card is completely taken up with his or her own mental and emotional processes. Or that their reserved attitude is telling you that you, yourself, need time to rediscover your own emotional roots.

6 **Each card represents both a motivation and a warning.**

A card such as the *Two of Cups* encourages us to share our feelings and exchange ideas, and at the same time it gives us a warning about half-hearted gestures (diluted feelings). The motivation and the warning are not necessarily mutually exclusive—in fact they may complement each other.

And this is true of every card: the *Tower* is at once an encouragement to open up and let oneself go, and also a warning against a lack of resolution or against pride (which comes before a fall!). The *Ten of Wands* cautions against having an exaggerated opinion of oneself and also against making unreasonable efforts; at the same time it can be an inspiration to give of one's best and to follow one's own inclinations, as the figure in the image is literally doing.

7 **Remember the symbolic nature of the images:**
Don't take everything at face value!

The *Pentacles* stand for money, but also for all that is material, for the body and generally for all the impressions and traits which we have gathered in the past and that we ourselves impress on others.

XIX - The Sun may have nothing to do with our local star! It is also a symbol for consciousness, for fatherhood or a divinity, for light, day and much more.

There is general consensus that the *Swords* represent, among other things, the weapons of the intellect. From this point of view, a card such as the *Six of Swords* has less to do with an actual boat or journey (although the image lends itself to such associations) than to a mental progression or process, to an intellectual connection between two (mental) territories, or to the search for a new 'shore'.

8 **Give yourself time to observe at leisure without jumping to conclusions.**

The *card of the day* provides the best way to train yourself into the habit of impartiality. Even though we would like the tarot to provide us with clear and especially quick answers to our current questions—and in fact precisely because of that—it is most helpful if we can exercise patience and first observe without trying to evaluate what the tarot card is providing in the way of insights.

Incidentally, this represents possibly the most important difference between beginners and more advanced users of the tarot: the novice thinks the card itself is the essential thing, whereas the old hand has learned that the way one looks at it is just as important.

The more we are prepared to immerse ourselves in the image—perhaps trying out different perspectives or adopting the figure's position or pose—the richer the harvest or the more unexpected the solution will be in the end.

9 **An interpretation is only complete after it has led to practical consequences.**

We will gain the greatest benefit from laying tarot cards when we are prepared not merely to seek theoretical insights, but also to draw practical conclusions. The practical results are the only yardstick with which we can assess whether a given interpretation was 'right' for our personal situation.

10 **Enjoy the magic of the moment.**

When laying card spreads we can enjoy two kinds of magic moment: on the one hand there is the magic of the images, the interplay of viewpoints and perspectives. And on the other hand the enchantment of time, its quality, its 'infinite momentariness'.

To enjoy the fascination of this mystery to the full, it helps to see every spread as something completely new and pristine, free from all past experiences. Of course, this doesn't mean we have to ignore all that has happened in the past—but it does mean allowing every card and every spread the chance to receive our open, unprejudiced attention, as if every time were the first time.

10 useful tips for interpretation

1 **The most important clues may be in the background.**

Many cards show a figure with a number of significant items behind his or her back. What happens behind one's back is, for oneself, something unseen, shadowy, something to which one has no conscious access (for instance, the vulnerable spot between Siegfried's shoulder-blades in the *Nibelungen saga).* We can only understand the full import of cards such as this when we take account of the fact that the figure in the image may be faced with a problem which he or she has not yet grasped. *We* can see what is behind their back, but the figure himself or herself may not be aware of it.

2 ***Pars pro toto* (the part stands for the whole).**

The little snail in the picture for the *Nine of Pentacles,* or the varying number of birds shown on the Swords court cards: These details have (both positive and negative) meanings which typify the card as a whole.

3 **The colors alone explain a great deal.**

white: the starting point (like a blank sheet of paper) or completion and healing; dazzle, emptiness or a new intellectual territory.

gray: unconscious state (in a psychological sense the 'shadow') or conscious indifference, i.e. equivalence or lack of prejudice.

black: the unknown, the earth's innards or the inner significance of a given situation, a 'black box', visible shadow, mental or emotional darkness or new territory.

red: heart, mentality or disposition, will, love, wrath, blood and soil.

yellow: consciousness, joie-de-vivre; envy, mental dissonance ('shrillness').

gold: sun, being conscious, eternity; envy, greed, dazzling, pomp.

orange: vitality, warmth, the mixture of red and yellow, arbitrariness.

blue: indifference, coolness, longing, the blues, sentimentality, inebriation

light blue: air, (open) sky / heavens; (clear) water, spirituality; also being 'blue-eyed', idolization.

green: freshness, youth, auspiciousness, inexperience, immaturity.

dark green: close to nature, vegetative, protracted, long-lasting.
beige: the human body, corporeality.
brown: down-to-earth, 'son-of-the-soil', grounded, of creation.
violet: borderline experience; the mixture of red and blue.

This brief outline provides the basic standard interpretations of the colors within the context of western culture and provides a reliable starting point for interpretation.

4 The color of the sky reveals a lot.

By taking account of the color of the sky on a given card you obtain a simple, but important clue for its interpretation.

5 Don't over-interpret numbers.

Numbers are there to be played with or for computing—they do not possess any generally valid inner significance. All-purpose statements like "the 5 stands for a crisis" or "a 6 always means harmony" are far removed from serious and dependable interpretation.

Of course, numbers can have a symbolic significance, such as is the case with '4711', '1945' or '9/11'.

And: a 1 can stand for uniqueness, but also for unity, single-mindedness, loneliness and all other terms in which oneness is to be found. Twoness can be found in words like twofold, twosome, double, twin etc. as well as in phrases: Two's company…, to double back, dual personality, etc.

Some numbers lend themselves to plays on words, e.g. "2 4 T"

Nevertheless, numbers do not carry any inherent, deeper meaning around with them. If the author of a book on interpretation writes, for instance, "The 5 is typical for a crisis, as the image shows…," this is no more than a projection of his own conviction onto the five of…card (i.e., that it necessarily has something to do with a crisis)—although the number five itself is quite innocent and certainly not shackled to the notion of crisis.

Generally, only the functional values of numbers have any significance in tarot interpretation, e.g. $2 + 3 = 5$. Advanced users of the tarot can try interesting exercises involving such methods[1].

[1] You can find some in: Evelin Burger/Johannes Fiebig: *The Complete Book of Tarot Spreads.* Sterling Publishing, New York City/NY

6 **Pay close attention to proportions.**

In the image of the *Four of Wands,* the figures are depicted much smaller than is the case in other images; they fall short. Or perhaps they are of normal height and are painted so small in order to emphasize the comparatively huge size of the wands. This sort of thing can be found in many other cards.

7 **Blind spots are gateways to new viewpoints.**

If you find that you can't help but regard a certain card in an especially positive or negative light, then you can be sure that you have discovered one of your blind spots. The same applies if you find a certain tarot deck generally very good, but with one or two cards you have a strong feeling that the artist has slipped up—this is usually a reliable indication of a blind spot.

Well then, lucky you! In situations like this it is practically always the case that the blind spot has arisen not just because of the tarot cards, but was already present in your life—the tarot has simply brought it out into the open. Now the important thing is to take your time. Give the blind spot the time it needs to come into focus. You will be rewarded by the new insights which this process brings.

8 **A card that does not portray a human figure has something to tell us.**

On some of the Rider/Waite Tarot cards no human beings are to be seen, e.g. on the *Eight of Wands* card. This is always a warning against losing oneself. And it always includes an impulse toward expanding one's consciousness in respect of processes than are greater than one's own person.

9 **Every single symbol is open to multiple interpretations.**

A wolf (as portrayed on *The Moon* card, for instance) can be a bad wolf symbolizing greed, voracity, rapacity, and an overpowering might (cf. the Grimm brothers' bad wolf), but equally it could be a sign for protective instincts and primeval forces (as in the collection of myths entitled *Women Who Run with the Wolves* by Clarissa Pinkola Estés.) And it is the same with every detail of each and every card.

That is why laying tarot cards practically cannot become boring, because one is constantly finding new interpretations of the cards and their symbols.

10 Court cards represent developed personalities.

A good way of achieving independence in interpreting the cards within a short space of time is to concentrate on the four suits (cf. page 28 f.). And when we regard the court cards (Queen, King, Knight and Page) as personalities that helps us to understand these four elements more fully.

Each court card represents an ideal type, a person who has complete and sovereign command over the element in question.

The individual court figures within a suit display specific character traits:

the Queen: impulsive, an initiator, an investigator (water type),

the King: thorough, intensive, consolidating (fire type),

the Knight: magnifying, expanding, a drawer of consequences (air type) and

the Page: makes something tangible out of or with the element in question (earth type).

An overview of the Major and Minor Arcanas

The four suits of Wands, Cups, Swords, and Pentacles contain 56 cards and together they constitute the so-called *Minor Arcana* (the word 'arcanum' means secret or mystery, and arcana is the plural). The fifth group comprises the 22 cards of the *Major Arcana*—the great mysteries—also known as the major stations of the tarot. Characteristic of the Major Arcana cards in the Rider / Waite deck is that they are the only ones headed with a number and having subtitles at the bottom.

Key terms related to the 22 Major Arcana cards

I - The Magician: One's own existence. Skills and potential.

II - The High Priestess: The inner voice, one's own opinion, the sense of one's own.

III - The Empress: Nature (and: naturalness, obviousness, spontaneity), fruitfulness, experience as a woman / with women.

IV - The Emperor: Self-determination, pioneer, experience as a man / with men.

V - The Hierophant: That which is holy in everyday matters.

VI - The Lovers: Paradise—lost and rediscovered.

VII - The Chariot: To tread one's own path—the way is the goal.

VIII - Strength: Wildness and wisdom. To accept oneself fully.

IX - The Hermit: To achieve order in one's life, to get things sorted out.

X - The Wheel of Fortune: Control of inner and outer change.

XI - Justice: Recognition of the other / others. One's true needs.

XII - The Hanged Man: Passion. Intense feelings.

XIII - Death: Letting go and reaping the harvest.

XIV - Temperance: The aims and plan for one's life. Solutions.

XV - The Devil: Establishing necessary taboos, breaking false ones.

XVI - The Tower: Liberation, fireworks, softening up calloused areas.

XVII - The Star: Soul star.

XVIII - The Moon: Return of what has been suppressed, release.

XIX - The Sun: A sunny spot, a state of consciousness.

XX - Judgement: The Day of Judgement is today.

XXI - The World: Old world and new world, outbreak, realization.

0 / XXII - The Fool: Naivety or completion, the absolute.

The 10 most important interpretations of the Wands

Element: Fire.

Basic meaning: Drives and deeds.

Concrete message: "Something has to happen!"

Practical realization: Move and be moved.

Key term: The will.

Psychological function (according to C. G. Jung): Intuition: instantaneous, holistic understanding.

The way of the Wands: purification, purgatory, the phoenix arising from the ashes.

The goal of the Wands: To burn! With passion and intensity a whole life long, to seek and find the true will, to surrender completely and in that way to recoup used-up energies.

Associations: The symbol of the phallus, the witch's broom, the root (and: the forebear), the offshoot (and: the descendant), twig, hiking stick, walking stick, cudgel.

Mottos: In the beginning was the deed. A man (woman) of action. How can I know what I want before I see what I do?

The 10 most important interpretations of the Cups

Element: Water.

Basic meaning: Feelings, longings, belief.

Concrete message: "It all depends on the inner convictions!"

Practical realization: Let it flow; to receive something or to let others receive.

Key term: The soul.

Psychological function (according to C. G. Jung): Feeling.

The way of the Cups: baptism, death and rebirth on a psychological level.

The goal of the Cups: To flow! To give water a set form, to give feelings their expression! The channel or the riverbank are constraints which cause the water within them to flow.

Associations: The female lap, the grail, chalices, the cup of cheer, bathtub, swimming pool; the ocean, showering, drinking etc.

Mottos: Water is the wellspring of all life. Everything is in a state of flow. Go with the flow.

The 10 most important interpretations of the Swords

Element: Air.

Basic meaning: The weapons of the intellect.

Concrete message: "This needs to be sorted out!"

Practical realization: Obtaining an intellectual grasp of an issue, ascertainment, assessment.

Key term: The mind.

Psychological function (according to C. G. Jung): Thought.

The way of the Swords: learning by experience.

The goal of the Swords: To make the burden lighter!

Associations: knightliness, gentility, maturity, swords to plowshares.

Mottos: Thinking is one of mankind's greatest pleasures. Knowledge without conscience is a sorry thing. He who has grasped his situation cannot readily be restrained.

The 10 most important interpretations of the Pentacles

Element: Earth.

Basic meaning: Talents (both coins and aptitudes / faculties).

Concrete message: "The proof of the pudding is in the eating!"

Practical realization: Either a given result is accepted—or it is rejected and a new one is sought.

Key term: The body, matter.

Psychological function (according to C. G. Jung): (sensory) perception.

The way of the Pentacles: multiplication of one's talents and harvesting the results.

The goal of the Pentacles: wealth and well-being!

Associations: thaler, dollar, the two sides of the coin, the impressions which we ourselves have experienced and which we make on others. The traces which we find and those which we make.

Mottos: The truth is what bears fruit. To have a talent and not to use it means to misuse it. We have inherited the earth from our parents and borrowed it from our children!

Important symbols and interpretations

The Major Arcana

The 10 most important symbols

Magic wand – ❶

One wand—two ends: 1 divides into 2 parts, and 2 poles become 1. The wand is itself a kind of parable: We can separate things and then recombine them in another way. **Also:** I, individuality, uniqueness.

Red mantle – ❷

Energy, passion, will, lifeblood (love, but also revenge, rage). **Positive:** to live for worthwhile goals and to live out one's heart's desire. **Negative:** base motives, egoism, only one's own will counts.

White robe – ❸

Like white light in which all the colors of the rainbow are combined: a new beginning and completion, achievement. **Positive:** lack of premeditation, innocence. **Negative:** gullibility, having to start over time and again.

Wand, Sword, Cup and Pentacle

Dowry, what life brings to you; tasks which are to be accomplished—**the tools of magic:** will, intellect, feelings, corporeality.

Table with markings – ❹

Workbench, reality, altar. **The present state of knowledge upon which the individual depends:** the inheritance from the past, traditional mysteries and solutions, present challenges and dormant treasures.

Roses and lilies

Again the themes of red and white (see the figure's clothing). **The rose garden—Positive:** a promise of happiness and success, transforming the earth into a garden. **Negative:** insisting on one's rights, isolation, loneliness.

Horizontal figure of eight (lemniscate) – ❺

Roller coaster. **Positive:** infinity, balance, perpetuum mobile, good vibrations, vitality, taking part in eternity. **Negative:** chasing one's tail, restlessness, repetition without progress.

Gestures of the arms – ❻

Above as below. The individual as connecting link between heaven and earth. Man as a channel. The relationship between possibility and reality. The successful union of thought and deed.

The serpentine girdle – ❼

Like the horizontal eight a sign of infinity, but also 'repetition without end'. Symbol for shedding what is no longer wanted, the permanent need for renewal. **But also:** poison, temptation, manipulation.

Yellow background

Sun, but also the search for meaning and envy, gold and greed. **Danger:** to get too close to the sun, enchantment can be dazzling. **Positive:** enlightenment also for the 'other' sides = reliable state of consciousness.

I - THE MAGICIAN

The card for uniqueness and singularity. You can do magical things too, and you will witness miracles. Every person is special and has his or her own individual claim on eternity. You, too, will achieve something that no-one else has ever managed before.

Make a difference!—Don't be good, be great!

■ Basic meaning

Today, magic has taken on an astonishingly personal significance: It no longer has much to do with props, tricks or an effort of will. We gather experiences on our own, independent path through life, ones which "no eye has yet beheld," and find or invent amazing solutions, time and again. This magic is unmistakable, but not supernatural. It is always available to us; it grows and flourishes with the successful development of our personal potential.

■ Spiritual experience

Becoming one with oneself, God, and the world: The universe loves you and needs you!

■ As the card for the day

Expand your horizons! Make use of all your opportunities!

■ As a prognosis / tendency

As long as we don't tread *our* own path, things seem to be jinxed. Put your own person in the center of your stage – find out about your talents and tasks.

■ For love and relationships

With God and in love all things are possible! With perseverance and ingenuity you can turn your world into a rose garden!

■ For success and happiness

Your ideas are your seed corn. Nobody else has the same ones and nobody can take them away from you.

The 10 most important symbols

The columns marked B and J – ❶

According to legend these are the columns of the ancient temple in Jerusalem: B and J stand for Beelzebub and Yahweh respectively. Also the initials of two principles named Boas and Jakim (corresponding with Yin and Yang).

The curtain

Is a dividing line between the individual and the wide ocean, and is at the same time permeable for reconnection. The work of the soul takes place on the inner screen onto which our inner images and dreams are projected.

Palm trees / pomegranate – ❷

Mark of that which is one's own, and also opening it up—sorting it according to B and J = the fruitfulness of spiritual life. This is what the palm and the pomegranate signify. Also, each is symbolic of sexuality, but behind the priestess' back.

The moon crown – ❸

The threefold moon or crown of Isis, the Egyptian mother goddess (to be seen in many depictions of the Madonna). **The three visible phases of the moon, the three stations of virginity, the adult woman and age.**

The Taurus horns / crescent moon – ❹

In the sign of Taurus the astrological moon is raised (especially potent). **The era of the matriarchs** = prehistory, Taurus age. **Moon today:** night, one's own, spirituality, the subconscious.

The scroll – ❺

The four letters awaken associations with the Torah as well as with a version of the word 'Tarot' (cf. *X-The Wheel of Fortune).* **Today:** the script for the course of one's own life.

The cross – ❻

Religion and spirituality. The region of the breast, the heart, is where the soul gathers impressions, sorts them, and generates personal opinions and inner values.

Great waters

Oceans of feeling, the flow of life, the circulation of water on the planet, ebb and flow. The figure in the image has two tasks: to take account of all this, and yet to keep what is private, her inmost life, separate.

The flowing robe

Positive: flowing, as water, in the rhythm of the moon and the tides. **Negative:** like the 'little mermaid'—half human, half sea creature.—Don't drown in emotions, but develop your own existence.

Light blue background

The heavens = The divine realm and the realm of the will. **Light blue** = (open) sky; (clear) water. **Positive:** lightheartedness, will, lucid mind. **Negative:** naivety, wishful thinking. **And:** out of the blue, the wide blue yonder.

II - THE HIGH PRIESTESS

History and legend relate of priestesses with oracular powers such as the Pythia of Delphi, the Sibyls (prophetesses), as well as Cassandra of Troy and temple women and nuns. Today we see them, just as all the other figures of the tarot, mainly as mirrors of our own personality. There's one in you, too!

Establish your own opinion—and live by it!

■ **Basic meaning**

Every person, every creature has his, her or its own value. The drape shown in the image symbolizes our inner screen on which we project all impressions and psychological events. At the same time, it stands for those hard and fast surroundings which we all need. Sometimes the task in hand is to create the space we need—and sometimes to open it up to the wider world.

■ **Spiritual experience**

Understanding the personal significance of thoughts, words or deeds through meditation or contemplation.

■ **As the card for the day**

Other people's advice won't help here. Stick to your own opinion.

■ **As a prognosis / tendency**

You are always your own soothsayer: What you think and believe is what becomes your reality—even if it comes from your imagination. So: Let the dead bury the dead and their obedience to old ways. Give yourself —and others—the chance to discover who you really are!

■ **For love and relationships**

The High Priestess' secret is her ability to perceive, sort out and put a name to feelings, needs and intuitions.

■ **For success and happiness**

Take heed of what your inner voice is telling you!

The 10 most important symbols

The figure's position or pose

Upright, majestic, self-confident, self-assured, relaxed, motivated, concentrated. The supposition that she may be pregnant contained in some interpretations is purely speculative. There are many kinds of fruitfulness.

Scepter / sign of Venus – ❶

The sign of Venus combines a circle and a cross = sun and earth, soul and body. Just this unity is typical for Venus and *The Empress*: with body and soul, **the unification of sense and the senses.**

The flowered robe – ❷

Flowers = the beauty of nature and a person's coming into bloom. The flowers are similar to the sign of Venus. **White, red, green:** the colors of *the Magician* and nature's green. Flowers to the people—bread and roses!

The gray heart – ❸

A great heart, calmly unprejudiced—all creatures and all impulses have a chance and a *raison d'existence*. If the heart is of stone, individuality degenerates into egoism which has no time for others.

Red throne on gray ground

Red and orange = life-blood and passion, the empress' emotionality. But this is surrounded by grayness. **Positive:** Impartiality. **Negative:** stones instead of bread, hardheartedness, lovelessness.

The crown of stars / laurels – ❹

The crown is decorated with 12 stars (as in many Madonna representations). **Taking stars from the sky and bringing them to fruition on the earth** (crown of laurels) is *the Empress'* task and gift (see sign of Venus).

Grain – ❺

The symbol of fruitfulness and reaping life's harvest. Nutrition (for body and soul), feeding and caring for oneself and others. Well-being, ease, sensuality, enjoyment, 'feeling good.'

Trees / Forest

Nature comes into its own: Every plant can find its place and have a chance to grow. "Living alone and free as a tree and brotherly as a forest, that is our yearning!" (Nazim Hikmet)

Waterfall – ❻

The river is connected with its source and at the same time it flows and falls. The Tower is not the only image associated with flying and falling! **The flow forward and the bond with the wellspring—both equally important!**

The color yellow

Sun, awareness of one's consciousness, the highest and holiest, search for meaning but also envy, gold, greed. **Danger:** back towards the sun = repression. **Positive:** lights up the 'other side' as well = reliable awareness.

III - THE EMPRESS

Burgeoning nature as shown in the image refers to the environment, but also to one's personal nature. Emotion, the expression of inner sentiment, is also typical of Venus in old mythology. Living these feminine aspects is not just women's work, but something for men to come to terms with as well.

The Empress and Goddess of Love within you.

■ Basic meaning

The term *The Empress* is redolent with royalty, majesty, sovereignty. And she also stands for the great goddess of antiquity, the threefold deity of Christianity and other religions, for the Mother of God such as Isis and Mary and not least for the goddess of love, variously named Astarte, Aphrodite or Venus. Finally, the card is a mirror of one's own femininity (and men's female aspects). She reflects one's personal experiences as a woman and/or with women, the inheritance of the mother, grandmother, and all female ancestors.

■ Spiritual experience

The enjoyment of the senses and sensuality.

■ As the card for the day

Take responsibility for your own well-being—take care of yourself! And ban false goddesses from your life.

■ As a prognosis / tendency

For your well-being: Invent rules that are good for you and stick to them!

■ For love and relationships

When we love and are loved our personal nature comes into bloom. Where sense and sensibility are given a chance to develop, love can grow and with it the beauty of being.

■ For success and happiness

The key: clarity, naturalness and satisfaction

The 10 most important symbols

Ankh / Key of Life / Crux Ansata – ❶

A hieroglyph (somewhat modified). **Stylized representation of the male reproductive organs**: the procreation of life, a symbol for the renewal of life. **In gold**: eternal life. Also a warning against greed.

Globus cruciger / golden apple – ❷

The cross-bearing orb = a symbol of power. A golden apple, mentioned in myths and legends, stands for eternal life and fertility. **Negative**: King Midas—his touch turned everything into gold, including his daughter.

Wasteland / New territory – ❸

The landscape: waste and void. **Negative**: wonderful fertility can wilt in the face of egoism and cruelty (gl. cruciger/golden apple). **Positive**: ruler = pioneer in a new land; he and only he can make the desert bloom.

Four rams' heads – ❹

Aries is the first sign of the zodiac, symbolizing **Eastertide, the springtime, the renewal of life.** The Christian Easter liturgy reflects this: "This land that was desolate has become like the garden of Eden" (Ezekiel 36:35).

The armor

Positive: well-prepared, chivalrousness. Respect, but also protection against others. **Negative**: elbow politics, the arrogance of power, pointless severity, unnecessary ballast, a colossus with feet of clay.

The river – ❺

The image is this: *The Emperor* must be and remain in the flow with himself and life. Only he who is prepared to change can remain true to himself. **The task is to start anew with the process of self-awareness once more.**

Black—white—red

Stages in alchemy: Black (under the throne) = unsolved problems and unused opportunities. White (beard and hair) = purity and wisdom. Red (the dominant color of the image) = new solution, illumination.

White beard / White hair

Symbol of power. Worldly wisdom, experience and permanence. But equally: a new beginning. The master is the true beginner—the master is the one who can assess the daily shifts in situations and the tasks in hand.

The gray throne – ❻

The rectangularity = the material world with its extension towards the four points of the compass. *The Emperor* stands for that facility within us **to find our place in the world** and then to rule over that place in our own right.

The golden crown – ❼

The closed crown symbolizes **one's own authority**; no higher powers are acknowledged. **Also**: the golden crown chakra; a golden head. **Gold** = consciousness, but also greed.

IV - THE EMPEROR

To be the ruler of one's own life; to be in control of oneself; to be the first; to face the unknown undaunted; to find a desert and transform it into a garden —all this is the might of the Emperor. And of course, it is available to women as well as to men!

The Emperor and god of spring within you.

■ Basic meaning

Emperor and king, Zeus, Jupiter and countless other father-figures can be associated with this image. It is a mirror of one's own virility (and a woman's male side). The card relates to one's own experiences as a man or with men, the inheritance of the father, grandfather and all male ancestors. *The Emperor* is that part of us which explores new possibilities in life. The ram (see throne) is the pioneer in us, the first sign of the zodiac, the absolute beginner.

■ Spiritual experience

"A man can stand anything if he can stand himself." (anon.)

■ As the card for the day

Wake up your pioneering spirit. Check out the scene. Accomplish things—for yourself.

■ As a prognosis / tendency

There is much to be gained by seeing this card not just as representative of an external order (family, state etc.) but also as a symbol of personal self-determination.

■ For love and relationships

Every relationship requires some hard work to master problems and discover new aspects of loving.

■ For success and happiness

Each person brings something new into the world. This newness needs a chance to develop.

The 10 most important symbols

The figures in the image

Gretchen's famous question: "What do you think of religion?" (Goethe's *Faust*) All three figures represent hierophants. Also, this image shows many details reminiscent of a Christian pope.

The gray columns – ❶

mark out a large building (academy, community of believers). **Danger:** petrification. **Opportunity:** sustainability. **Gray =** indifference and the unconscious; or neutrality, equanimity and tolerance.

The tiara / Threefold crown – ❷

The papal crown. The Pope is held to be God's representative on earth: The term *pontifex maximus* means great bridge-builder! **The threefold crown stands for this bridge to the threefold deity.**

The threefold bishop's staff – ❸

A shepherd's crook. A bishop's staff has two crosses. Three crosses one above the other are reserved for the Pope as spiritual leader. So here the card is telling us **not to be sheep, but shepherds!**

The key – ❹

Jesus used the symbol of the key to authorize Peter: "I will give you the keys of the kingdom of heaven; and whatever you bind on earth shall be bound in heaven, and whatever you loose on earth shall be loosed in heaven."

The trinity

Visible several times in the image. **Religious meaning:** the divine trinity. **Also:** the cult of the great goddess (virgin, mother, queen). 3 worlds (heaven, earth, underworld); 3 consciousness levels (superego, ego, id).

The tonsure – ❺

Shaving the hair from the upper part of the head is practiced to this day in some orders of monks, and it is supposed to signify a spiritual openness toward God.

Lilies and roses

As with *the Magician* and some other cards, these two flowers in red and white signify purity and love, the basis of every true religion.

The blessing – ❻

As above, so below. One part is visible, the other not. As in heaven, so on the earth. Not only priests have the power to sanctify, but any worthwhile act is a blessing.

The quintessence

The V of the card and the five fingers of the hand which blesses indicate the *quintessence*, the essentials (literally, *the fifth essence*). Strengths and weaknesses are a gift of God. What counts is what you make of them.

V - The Hierophant

This Greek word means 'he who proclaims what is sacred'. In some schools of initiation, the high priest is referred to as the hierophant. The card is a reminder of such rituals generally and the popes of the Catholic church (and originally the whole Christian church). As with every card—use it as a mirror!

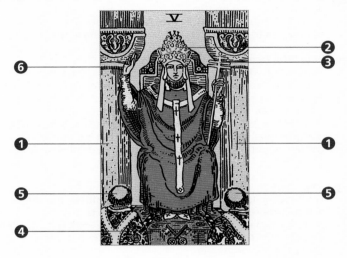

The key is in your hands!

■ Basic meaning

What was once the task of the priests and the high priest now devolves upon us all: How can we find personal answers to the great and little mysteries of life? How can we organize our high days and holidays (holy-days)?

Both the main and the minor figures in the image symbolize our personal strengths and weaknesses—together they lead to the quintessence, to the divine spark, to that which is holy in every human being (and which is often bottled up and stowed away).

■ Spiritual experience

Every person who reveals what is sacred is a spiritual teacher for everybody else.

■ As the card for the day

Share your secrets with others and open yourself up to their needs.

■ As a prognosis / tendency

This is how you come to grasp the sense of your life. What makes sense vitalizes the senses.

■ For love and relationships

Which events, which days of the year, which turning points in life have been of significance to yourself and those close to you? Sanctify these great and little occasions with reverence and devotion. There is nothing more important in your life.

■ For success and happiness

The key: one's own competence.

The 10 most important symbols

Paradise—old and new

Eve seduced Adam with the apple, and God banned them from paradise. What many don't know: The concept of paradise regained on the day of judgment is equally firmly rooted in the Christian tradition.

The tree of life / The tree of knowledge – ❶

Irrespective of the story of paradise, the two trees are indicative of the polarity of life, especially of the principles of female and male gender, nature and the will, earth and fire.

The angel – ❷

The angel builds a bridge between these poles and provides a link to the Highest, to God. **Positive:** a symbol for greater personal potential. **Negative:** high-flyer, observer, know-all, hopeless idealist.

The displacement – ❸

Rainer-Maria Rilke: "A wonderful life together (...): If people (...) could appreciate the distance between themselves, (...) they would be able to see each other wholly and in front of the backdrop of the wide heavens."

The nakedness

Negative: lack of shame, shamelessness, crudity. **Positive:** openness, honesty and—last but not least—eroticism and lust. The card No. VI is also *the* main tarot card for sexuality.

The cloud – ❹

The cloud and the angel are like an intermediate instance between the sun and the lovers. The grayer the cloud is, the less one can see through it and the more the two lovers below are standing in the shadows.

The shadow

This corresponds to the psychological term shadow, which comprises those parts of our personality which are there, but we cannot see them. This can easily lead to trouble—out of the blue!

The sun

Positive: the angel connects the humans with the Highest. **Negative:** with the cloud, the angel forms a *barrier* between the humans and the sun: through unclear ideals, gray thoughts, obscure aims.

The mountain – ❺

As a warning it can mean: a mountain of difficulties between the lovers which needs to be overcome. **In a positive sense** it can be a sign of their common high-point experiences, of being on top of the world.

The snake – ❻

Warns against low instincts and motivation. However, with its coils it also indicates development, wisdom gained through experience.

VI - THE LOVERS

Many people know the story of Adam and Eve's expulsion from Paradise, but its counterpart is less well known: The bible and other traditions also tell of the return to Paradise, of eternal life which begins on the Day of judgment. Well, when is the Day of Judgment? Today, of course!

The greatest moments in life…

■ Basic meaning

We all thirst after love, and still we are sometimes afraid of loving or being loved.

As long as we keep searching for our better half we are in danger of cutting ourselves in two. Or the search for agreement: There is only one person who can truly understand you—and that person is yourself. There is no point in expecting your partner to do what you can better do yourself. Nor that he or she should provide what only God can give: spiritual peace, release, fulfillment.

■ Spiritual experience

The sun's rays disperse the shadow…

■ As the card for the day

"Love yourself, and then you can marry anybody." (Eva-M. Zurhorst)

■ As a prognosis / tendency

Love is a matter of choice: He/She who loves gets more of everything in life than somebody who doesn't!

■ For love and relationships

In the end, love becomes emancipated from its traditional roles in relationships and the family and returns to what it always was: the new paradise…

■ For success and happiness

Love begins and stays through common creations. Without added value, i.e. something productive which arises out of it, a relationship cannot last for very long.

The 10 most important symbols

The sphinxes – ❶

The sphinxes stand for life's mysteries. Note that the sphinxes are not pulling the chariot—there is no drawbar. They are simply running ahead: Today's puzzles are tomorrow's path.

The chariot of stone – ❷

The cube represents the 'karma' of the space-time which we occupy in this life. We cannot simply 'drop out' of our personal destiny, but we can certainly affect the direction in which it is heading.

The charioteer with laurels – ❸

The upper part of the chariot stands for our subjectivity—for everything that we can and must decide for ourselves.

Crown of stars and canopy of stars – ❹

The infinity of space, the beauty and order of the cosmos. **Also:** a symbol of liberty and independence as well as one's personal truth (cf. *XVII - The Star*).

The moon figures – ❺

The polarity of the soul represented by laughing and crying. The chariot stands for the internal and external experiences that we gather in our path through life and which form our personality.

The armor

'Hard on the outside, soft on the inside'—protected, armored, ready and prepared for the next development. **Also:** the persona, outer façade, or even protective shield that we present to the outside world.

Magic wand / hiking staff

Also a sign of preparedness and being well-equipped, of wayfaring and confidence, relying on one's own efforts. A sign of the magic powers *(The Magician)* which are with us in all walks of life.

The winged sun – ❻

Ancient sign of the great sun god. This is the snitch in the Harry Potter stories —the difference between victory and defeat. Here: the symbol of the inner center, the personal sun to accompany us on life's journey.

Lingam and Yoni – ❼

A traditional Indian representation of the male and female sexual organs. In this context the accent is not so much on the sexual aspect, but generally on balancing out opposites. It is often seen as a top, another possibility!

City, land, river

In the background, Father City and Mother Nature are visible. As ever, the main figure may be unaware of what is going on behind his/her back = danger of denial of or ignorance about one's own origins.

VII - THE CHARIOT

The Chariot stands for the experience of one's own personality, which is formed through both conscious effort (the charioteer) and the drives of the unconscious, karma, the story of one's life (the stone chariot). The sphinxes represent the mysteries of life.

Daring to steer one's own course.

■ Basic meaning

The riddle of the sphinx in front, Father City and Mother Nature behind, the stars above, duties and pleasures on the shoulders—the best way to balance out all these different issues is to formulate one's wishes clearly! The way of the wishes is the way to fulfillment of meaningful desires—dispensing with unjustified fears. As long as you are on this path, everything you do is worthwhile. Equally, the greatest achievements are valueless if they do not serve to further your progress on the way of your wishes.

■ Spiritual experience

The path is its own goal.

■ As the card for the day

Nothing ventured, nothing gained—get clear what you want, and then live your life accordingly.

■ As a prognosis / tendency

You cannot 'get off' your chariot, your karma. But you can send it in a different direction.

■ For love and relationships

A good card to get some fresh air into a relationship: Give yourself and your partner each a free wish!

■ For success and happiness

Cultivate your own tastes—preferences and habits that do you good. Abide by your own judgment wholeheartedly.

The 10 most important symbols

The figures' positions or poses

 The white woman runs the fingers of her right hand through the lion's mane; her left hand rests upon its maw. Both have arched backs. **Positive:** taking care and caring about. **Negative:** dependency.

The red lion – ❶

 An ancient symbol not only of impulsive power and fire, but also for the will and especially the true will. One of the highest symbols in early modern alchemy. Cultivation of the will.

The white woman – ❷

 The white/wise woman, the wisdom of nature, innocence that tames wildness. The lion tamer who challenges and strengthens the forces which reside in this planet and in each one of us.

The lion's mouth – ❸

 in the woman's lap: vitality, lust and sexuality unite the basics of humanity: wildness and wisdom, instinct and intellect, self-preservation and self-propagation, which makes demands and gives strength.

Woman and animal I

 Here we see a primeval image: the beauty and the beast, King Kong and the white woman, the princess and the animal husband (in legend)—all pictures of the redemption of nature as well as the need for it.

Woman and animal II

 All of the transient, / Is parable, only: / The insufficient, / Here, grows to reality: / The indescribable, / Here, is done: / Woman, eternal, beckons us on. (final words in Goethe's *Faust*)

The floral crowns

 Flowers = beauty of every single creature's soul. To make a garden of the earth, where each flower can bloom in its own essence. The flower-power card.

The horizontal eight – ❹

 Roller coaster. **Positive:** infinity, equilibrium, permanent movement, good vibrations, vitality, being part of eternity. **Negative:** chasing one's tail, restlessness, repetition without progress.

The blue mountains – ❺

 Positive: creating heaven on earth; peak experiences, ecstasy. **Negative:** the blue mountains are behind the figure. You'd better look around you.

The yellow sky

 Sun, but also the search for meaning and envy, gold and greed. **Danger:** getting too close to the sun can cause blindness. **Positive:** illumination of the darker sides as well = reliable consciousness.

VIII - Strength

The white/wise woman and the red lion address the archetypal beauty and the beast theme. Each one's release/salvation is dependent on that of the other. Thus this card also describes a personal culture in which we succeed in letting creative powers flourish.

The Beauty and the Beast—you have both of them inside you!

■ Basic meaning

The red lion and the white woman represent the strongest sides of human nature: As the personification of wildness and wisdom they increase our vitality and *joie-de-vivre*. And at the same time they warn us about their unconscious versions, known as *anima* and *animus*. These express themselves in animal instincts and wild thoughts which swirl under the surface. Think about the Sorcerer's Apprentice, who had no idea what he was saying and bringing about.

■ Spiritual experience

As above, so below: Man—and woman—have two centers of lust: one between the legs and one between the ears!

■ As the card for the day

Fulfillment is being present to the full, concentrating all one's strength to focus on the moment.

■ As a prognosis/tendency

The key to potency is the recognition and reconciliation of strengths and weaknesses.

■ For love and relationships

Forget useless ideals and half-hearted activity. Give the Force a new chance!

■ For success and happiness

To live in the fullness of one's strength is to be completely present at a given moment. So this card is also the card for high points and peak sexual experiences (see blue mountains)—as well as in every other walk of life.

The 10 most important symbols

The figure's position or pose

His gaze is directed both inwards and outwards. His attention may be directed here—or elsewhere. His hue is gray, but he himself brings light and color. His beard is an old man's, but the snow symbolizes newness, virginity.

Lantern and nightwatchman I – ❶

Traditionally an ambivalent symbol: On the one hand the nightwatchman stands for vigilance in the dark hours. On the other hand he is associated with sleepiness and inactivity during the day (cf. nightwatchman state).

Lantern and nightwatchman II

In the biblical parable of the wise and foolish virgins, only the wise virgins remember to take extra oil for their lamps. They are prepared for the arrival of the bridegroom.

The six-pointed star – ❷

The hexagram, the Star of David, which today forms part of Israel's national flag. Here, however, it has no political connotations, but is **a sign of the conjunction of two triangles (heaven and earth), the divine light within us.**

The golden-yellow stave – ❸

The light coming from the lantern determines the color of the stave. And this light is the **light and strength** which every person brings into the world with his or her individual personality.

The gray clothing

This color, or its absence, warns against uncertainty and lack of personal development. It gives an impulse to be more objective, while recognizing that one's own light and path (the stave) are more important than outer flamboyance.

The green-gray sky

Together with the gray garment, the color of the sky also expresses withdrawal from **outside distraction and concentration on what is essential**—one's own light and the golden stave, the divine spark!

The white beard – ❹

The beard has a long tradition as a symbol of potency. Sometimes, too, it is an expression of disguise, of hiding behind a self-wrought thicket. **The white beard = the wisdom of age, fulfillment and a fresh start (cf. snow).**

The snow – ❺

To have forgotten a part of oneself, or even to have let it freeze over. **Or:** snow as a metaphor (like a sheet of white paper) for **fulfillment and a new beginning:** A sign that one has successfully dealt with a problem!

Position of the figure in the picture

As the white snow is an image for healing the earth and revering it, so does the raised position on a knoll stand for the vantage point from which one can review one's life and **make peace with oneself, with God and with all!**

IX - THE HERMIT

It is over simplistic to limit the significance of The Hermit to his being a symbol for isolation or forlorn loneliness. He has more to tell us, something which is of special importance to you: The Hermit is one who deals with his problems when the time is ripe and without trying to avoid the issue.

Hold your lamp at the ready…

■ Basic meaning

Seeing a hermit's life as no more than asceticism and renunciation misses the point. Historical reports about hermits always contain references to living a life in the experience of God, in His presence. In all the various religions, this condition is seen as a metaphor to describe the highest possible state of bliss. In other words, what the uninitiated sees as being no more than relinquishment and sacrifice is for the hermit himself the key to transcendental happiness. This aspect may help you to see your own current situation in a new light.

■ Spiritual experience

An independent path to and with God.

■ As the card for the day

Sometimes this card signals that it is time to withdraw, but more often it gives us a hint to make calm but steady efforts to throw off unimportant ballast and concentrate on the essentials.

■ As a prognosis / tendency

You will pay off debts, both in the material as well as moral sense. And that will do you good!

■ For love and relationships

A good card for addressing existing problems and getting them sorted out!

■ For success and happiness

In your current situation, go for solutions that bring lasting results—don't put things off until tomorrow; start tackling the issues today.

The 10 most important symbols

The sphinx with sword – ❶

The sphinx = mythical mystery consisting of (among other things) the four elements Fire, Water, Air and Earth: As a reflection of the image as a whole, the sphinx is an expression of unity in diversity.

The snake Typhon or Seth – ❷

During the late period in Ancient Egypt, the god Seth came to be seen as the **personification of evil and destruction.** His Greek name is Typhon. Here, **he is indicative of the negative or downward principle.**

The god Anubis – ❸

Anubis = Egyptian god with the head of a dog or jackal who accompanies souls on their way to re-incarnation. **He stands for the positive, constructive principle.** Seth and Anubis = the ups and downs of fate.

Four elements / Four evangelists – ❹

Luke, the bull—earth; Mark, the lion—fire; John, the eagle—water (sequence of symbols scorpion—snake—eagle); Matthew, the angel or youngling—air. Many other equivalences.

The Latin characters

T–A–R–O: These letters can be used to form the following Latin sentence: *ROTA TARO ORAT TORA ATOR:* The wheel of tarot proclaims the law of Hathor (the Egyptian goddess of destiny).

The Hebrew characters

Y–H–V–H: the tetragram-maton (having four letters), the unutterable name of God **Y–A–H–W–E–H** or **J–E–H–O–V–A.** **Also:** the four elements: Y = fire; H = water and also earth; V = air.

The alchemistic characters

As in the corners, as in the sphinx, here too we see the four elements: Mercury (above) = air; sulfur (right) = fire; water (below) = water; salt (left) = earth.

The threefold circle

We see three circles (together with the center, the hub, there are four stages of expansion). Again, it has to do with **multiplicity and unity, with the inner and outer worlds, microcosm and macrocosm.**

The spokes and hub of the wheel

The spokes are paths from the inside to the outside and vice versa. **The double task:** On the one hand to grow beyond oneself and discover the world. On the other hand to withdraw into oneself and find one's inward self.

Book and wings – ❺

Human beings are the only creatures that can learn from the experiences of others! Existing solutions, one's own and others' experiences of success and failure are the stuff of which we make our own wings.

X - Wheel of Fortune

Happiness needs to be found and recognized. That is the meaning of the opened books: It is less a matter of scholarship than of enlightenment, one's own view of the world, understanding interrelationships—so that we can recognize opportunity and fulfillment in what fate provides.

Happiness is having a talent for fate. (Novalis)

■ Basic meaning

The sphinx is a being which is composed of elementary parts: a bull's torso (earth), lion's paws and tail (fire), an angel / human face (air) and eagle's wings (here, the wings have been replaced by the sword; water). Diversity and unity, continuity and change—all this is expressed by the sphinx alone. The remaining languages and symbols echo and magnify this message—the image is full of surprising examples of diversity and unity on many levels.

■ Spiritual experience

Happiness is waiting to be found—and often it is simply handed to us!

■ As the card for the day

Keep an eye out for connections between various areas of life. Make a collage of it!

■ As a prognosis / tendency

Cooperating with fate starts with the welcoming—albeit cautious—acceptance of 'coincidences' as they occur. A great time is starting for you!

■ For love and relationships

Taking a look beyond one's own fence helps to develop tolerance for one's partner—and more room to maneuver when you happen not to be able to understand him / her!

■ For success and happiness

The time is ripe for bigger dimensions and better solutions!

The 10 most important symbols

The figure's position or pose

As with *The Magician*, the position of the arms expresses the principle as above, so below (especially when the arms are prolonged with the scales and sword). A channel that connects heaven and earth with each other.

Scales and sword – ❶

Classical weapons of the intellect. Scales = assess and ascertain. The sword = instrument for implementing a judgment, but also for arriving at one: the case is split up for further investigation and analysis.

Libra and desire – ❷

Successful wishing can only be developed through choices and knowing the alternatives. Is that why the scales and what is weighed (libra) are linked to freedom (*liber*, liberty) and lust (love, libido) in many languages?

The red robe – ❸

Dealing consciously (using the weapons of the intellect) with drives and emotions (represented by the dominating red of the robe): Either mental control and censure or conscious indulgence of pleasure!

Red—white—green – ❹

Red (with violet, see below) and gray dominate: heart and intellect. **The yellow-green mantle** stands for naturalness and growth and warns against immaturity. **A small patch of white (the brooch):** a little openness.

The three and four of the crown – ❺

More than just decoration: The three battlements of the crown and the quadratic jewel below them are a play on threesomeness and foursomeness **as the epitomes of the feminine and masculine, spiritual and material worlds.**

The third eye – ❻

The jewel is a reference to the third eye (as in the card *Two of Swords*). It stands for **higher intuition and for the resolution of contradictions.**

Gray columns / Gray floor

Gray is the color of neutrality, equanimity, and tolerance, and on the other hand, of indifference and lack of awareness. The danger of fossilization and the opportunity to achieve sustainability!

The violet curtain

In the spectrum of colors, violet lies closest to invisible radiation. The sword extends beyond the curtain, a sign of the sensibility and sensitivity which are needed here. The scales give a measure to what was uncertain.

The yellow background

The violet curtain borders shining yellow: **Negative:** the sun, clear consciousness, is obscured by rules and regulations. **Positive:** overeagerness, envy, delusion, greed (= yellow) are curbed by them.

XI - JUSTICE

Here we have to do with a borderline experience which makes clear to us that there is something greater than ourselves. Justice is no abstract term, but a practical answer to the question as to how we can satisfy and take account of our own needs as well as those of others.

The more precise the inquiry, the more compassionate the judgement!

■ Basic meaning

'Justice' is not an abstract principle, but the practical question as to how you can reconcile all the wishes and fears present—how you can take account of the experiences and needs of all concerned. The dominant red is the color of lifeblood, the libido (the energy of the drives), an expression of love, the will, aggression or anger. The scales and the sword stand for careful consideration and assessment, for the conscious weighing-up and treatment of great passions.

■ Spiritual experience

Wise judgment depends on the 'righteousness' of the heart!

■ As the card for the day

Find out what everybody's needs are!

■ As a prognosis / tendency

"Our experiences generally mutate quickly into judgments. We remember these judgments, but think they are the experiences. Of course, judgments are not as reliable as experiences. A special technique is needed in order to keep experiences fresh, so that one can continually extract new judgments from them." (B. Brecht)

■ For love and relationships

Go for fairness in every relationship.

■ For success and happiness

Have the courage to criticize, and also the courage to praise.

The 10 most important symbols

The figure's position or pose I

 The image is based on Germanic-Celtic legend. Both the god Odin and the great magician Merlin each spend days and nights in this position. Shamanic rituals, too, include the process of hanging.

The figure's position or pose II

 Arms and head = triangle; the legs form a sign of the cross and an inverted four. Together, the triangle and cross = **alchemistic sign for fire:** sulfur (cf. *X-Wheel of Fortune*), i.e. also a fiery station.

T-cross/Tau-cross I – ❶

 The Greek letter tau (Latin T) is composed of vertical and horizontal lines like this. **The tau-cross is also the symbol for the famed Saint Francis of Assisi** who said: "What you seek is that which seeks."

T-cross/Tau-cross II

 Negative: the horizontal beam limits the development of the vertical one; passivity or fatalism restricts one's higher potential. **Also:** T as a sign for 'Break!' as well as for 'dead end!'

T-cross/Tau-cross III

Positive: the final stage of development has been reached and come to a crowning conclusion. **Tau-cross = the greatest happiness, magnificence and the ultimate feeling!**

The height

 The hanged man has a definite point of view—which is based not on the earthly perspective, but the heavenly one. **A sur-real world—literally a world above reality.**

The hanging – ❷

 The card warns against many kinds of dependency. It also encourages us to take a break from time to time (chill out, hang around). But first of all it is an inspiration to depend on what one believes.

The radiant crown – ❸

 He who depends with his whole existence upon that which he considers to be holy experiences the highest reaches of spiritual strength. **The halo (Latin: *nimbus*) is a symbol for potentates, enlightened ones or saints.**

The cord around the right foot – ❹

 The right leg = conscious side: It is a matter of passion and belief to which we consciously devote ourselves. **Warning:** against the snares of overzealous martyrdom and disabling obsessions.

The inversion

 One way or another: We also depend on our beliefs. All the more important that these should not be superstitious or without faith. There is a need for phases of scrutiny in which we turn ourselves and our values upside down.

XII - The Hanged Man

The Hanged Man has a perfectly normal, clear and unequivocal point of view—only his point of reference is not the earth, not defined in earthly terms. His 'standpoint' is the heavenly, transcendental perspective.

■ Basic meaning

The Hanged Man believes in what he *depends* on, and he depends on what he believes, which is a tragedy when it turns out that the belief is superstition. So the essential thing is to examine one's own beliefs. To do this it is sometimes necessary to stand on one's head. Alternatively, of course, the image can also be a pointer to inappropriate passivity, to a person who simply hangs around.

■ Spiritual experience

Metanoeite—Greek for: *Turn back and change yourselves!* (A slogan of Francis of Assisi, whose emblem is a T-cross.)

■ As the card for the day

Take a good look at the points that your suppositions depend on.

■ As a prognosis / tendency

One way or another, this is the end of the road—passion that either bears witness to a great story of suffering or an uplifting ardor.

■ For love and relationships

The head is at the lowest point here, the body above it. This can be an indication of another kind of wisdom which can only be attained when one surrenders oneself.

■ For success and happiness

A change of consciousness brings you a completely new perspective on the world.

The 10 most important symbols

The black rider – ❶

This card is a mirror, too: It is not just a question of letting go, but also actively bringing something to a conclusion. Warns against harshness and unjustified aggression; encourages positive, consistent action.

The white horse – ❷

The horse symbolizes strength, vitality, and subconscious drives. The color white stands for completion and a new beginning. The contrast between black and white is a reminder of great extremes in life.

Standard with harvest crown – ❸

The great flower consisting of five ears of grain (pentagram, downward-pointing) makes one thing very clear: **it is harvest time!** The Reaper's task is not to destroy but to bring in the harvest!

The king without a crown – ❹

The death of the ego, the end of worldly might. **Negative:** loss of control, impotence. **Positive:** doffing one's headgear out of respect for the laws of life and death as an aspect of *the Emperor's* rule over himself.

The bishop without a Staff – ❺

Positive: the final stage of development has been reached and come to a crowning conclusion. Tau-cross = greatest happiness, magnificence and the ultimate feeling!

The girls / children – ❻

The larger girl turns away. Only the small child and the priest face *Death* itself. As adults we have to be children or priests in order to accept death as being a normal part of life.

The ship of the souls – ❼

An image from Egyptian mythology to be found reflected in many religions: **The boat which carries the souls from death to reincarnation.** Thus this card also stands for the changing phases of life.

The heavenly gate – ❽

"Knocking on heaven's door": Death is not simply the end. In fact, it is quite possible to be 'dead' long before one dies—and live on long after having died.

The eternal city – ❾

An image from the New Testament: The eternal city (or eternal Jerusalem) is the paradise which shall return on the day of judgment. Well—today is the day of judgment! And death and change are today's issues.

The gray sky

The golden sun may be rising or going down. The gray sky warns against indifference and apathy— in this case in respect of death as part of life. And it is an inspiration towards a calm, unruffled spirit.

XIII - Death

Something comes to an end. When something pleasant comes to an end, we are sad—and conversely glad when something awful stops. But the image also reminds us: There is still something left to do. You need your 'positive aggression'—the strength to bring about necessary and radical change.

Let go in order to bring in the harvest: The Reaper is ready to do his work!

■ **Basic meaning**

Sadness in the face of death and loss is unavoidable, but don't try to suppress a fear of death. One can die before one dies—and still be alive long after death! In any case the meaning of death is not nothingness: The Reaper wishes to bring in a harvest—here the black rider bears a harvest crown on his standard.

■ **Spiritual experience**

"And as long as you do not have this: Die and be reborn!
You are but a dreary guest
On this dark earth."
(Goethe)

■ **As the card for the day**

Which fruits are ripe to pluck—which results are still missing? What is no longer fitting for you?

■ **As a prognosis / tendency**

The effects of one's own life continue to make themselves felt beyond death. All the more urgent is thus the question as to what you plan to experience, form and harvest during this life.

■ **For love and relationships**

Make space for a new sunrise.

■ **For success and happiness**

If a life is to bear fruit the conditions must be prepared for the harvest in the appropriate sequence. But it is never too late to begin.

The 10 most important symbols

An angel on earth

The angel is the only figure in the picture. Here there is no way around the need to get to grips with one's heavenly potential. It has to do with one's higher self—but also with unrealistic idealism.

The breastplate / The amulet – ❶

The triangle stands for femininity and spirituality; the square for masculinity and matter: bringing their opposite aspects into a state of productive tension. (Above the amulet: the four Hebrew letters J-H-V-H.)

Mixing / Liquefaction – ❷

Contradictions are resolved and reconciled by creating a potential difference between them so that things can flow. Finding the right measure also means achieving the right state of tension and balance of opposites.

The three levels – ❸

Below: the poles (land and water) still unreconciled. **In the middle:** the contradictions find a relationship to each other— the flow begins. **Above:** unity (the third eye) and a complete span of differences (large wings).

The lengthy path – ❹

The legendary true will, life's plan. **Aim:** the right tasks in life which we bring to a favorable conclusion—and which bring us there too! **A warning** against long-windedness, false ideals, and complicated procedures.

The blue water

The blue of the water reappears in the blue of the mountains. Spirituality (mind and soul) which determines both the origin and the goal. The light blue warns us against naivety and wishful thinking.

The blue mountains – ❺

Symbol for the *marriage of heaven and earth*, the mystery of unification which runs through this card. **Practical exercise:** seek and find your own destiny in the lifestyle which best harmonizes with your personal self.

The sun / third eye – ❻

The head of the angel and the sun above the mountains have a similar form—they are intended to correspond with each other. When the personal will and the will of fate come together, great things are possible!

The gray sky

But: The sun is at the figure's back. **A warning** against unnoticed, forgotten intentions. The gray sky warns against indifference in respect of life's goals, and it encourages us to adopt a neutral attitude.

Fire wings – ❼

The wings exceed the limits of the image: new possibilities are always there; there is no end in sight. **Negative:** purgatory, perfectionism, flight into delusion. **Positive:** purging; combining the infinite with the necessary!

XIV - TEMPERANCE

Even in ancient times, temperance was considered to be one of the cardinal virtues. The themes are finding the right measure and aiming for the highest goals in life. The card is an invitation to grasp the contradictions of life with both hands.

Changing the world—and having fun doing it…

■ Basic meaning

The alchemists referred to *the mysterium coniunctionis* (the secret of union), which they regarded as the aim of the great work *(opus magnum)*, as the *marriage between heaven and earth*.

The greatest works, however, are lifelong tasks. This is portrayed in the long road—undertakings which are so large that they take up a whole lifespan; goals which awaken the angel within you—your higher self—your great potential, and bring it to fruition!

■ Spiritual experience

We continue to experience purgatory—a process of refinement—as long as the right measure has not been found.

■ As the card for the day

Grasp the true contradictions of your life with both hands…

■ As a prognosis / tendency

…for that will enable you to see things as they are and—not in spite of that, but precisely because of it—that will help your personal will to achieve its aim.

■ For love and relationships

Your deeds create new facts—and through them you recreate yourself time and again. It is important to let your partner participate in the process.

■ For success and happiness

Set up a creative workshop in your daily routine—where you can regularly replenish your spiritual reservoir.

The 10 most important symbols

The figure's position or poses

 Parallels with *VI-The Lovers* and *V-The Hierophant* are obvious. Maybe the two 'Lovers' have spent time and energy hauling the great statue of the devil on its stone plinth out of the darkness.

The horns – ❶

 A sign of uncivilized nature. They signify not so much unfaithfulness (often associated with the horn image) as with everything in us which remains original and unrefined—which can be a curse or a blessing.

The bat's wings / claws – ❷

 Bat: an animal of great sensitivity, nocturnal, well able to orientate itself in the dark. **The taloned feet:** bird, element air. The devil as an earth-spirit!

The triangular head – ❸

 The downward pointing pentagram warns against negative energy that pulls everything down with it. It is an invitation to find a personal quintessence which points downward, i.e. is grounded.

The goat's haunches – ❹

 Let go of prejudices! The goat symbolizes the drives and instincts which every animal has. Don't brand anybody as a scapegoat. **Equally:** follow your own instincts.

The cube – ❺

 A symbol for the material. The black cube (the holy of holies in some religions, e.g. the Kaaba in Mecca): in the western world a symbol of un-worked material and the unexplored self.

The chains – ❻

 warn against dependency, especially in the form of a vicious circle. **Positive:** however, this is the card associated with yoga (literally: 'yoke'). **Voluntariness:** the chains lie loose. Acceptance of material bonds.

The torch

 Stands for our mission to **bring light into the darkness**—that means differentiating between positive and negative (e.g. attraction and repulsion). The 'devil', though, mixes them up at first.

The symbols on the hand – ❼

 The opposite or the extension of The *High Priest's* sign of blessing. Here: all fingers opened up = everything is openly visible. We look into a black box and discover hitherto unknown yearnings—or garbage.

The tails – ❽

 Like the horns: man came down from heaven to the earth not only as an angel, but also as an ape from the trees. **The task is to acknowledge and fashion what remains of our primordial nature.**

XV - The Devil

As soon as this card appears it is clear that the threshold of the 'taboo' has been crossed. What was hitherto surging under the surface is now visible. And that is the advantage and the challenge at once.

Are you on the horns of a dilemma?

■ Basic meaning

On the one hand the devil represents a kind of *vampire*, a truly burdensome torment of which we have good reason to be afraid. We can get rid of this aspect of the darkness when we finally come to recognize him.

In a quite different sense the devil personifies a *deprived child*. That is a part of us which we have so far treated with neglect—even though we secretly, and justifiably, have a certain longing for it. Now is the time to redress this.

■ Spiritual experience

"Bring light into the darkness and you will find a lot of old junk—and new treasures!"

■ As the card for the day

You have the opportunity to knock off a pair of old horns.

■ As a prognosis / tendency

When you bring light into the darkness, the vampire falls to dust and the deprived child in your cellar takes on form and color.

■ For love and relationships

It is not a sign of disaster and certainly nothing to be ashamed of—in fact it is usually a sign of quality—when the problematical aspects of a relationship come out into the open.

■ For success and happiness

Take all the time you need in order to face the unknown und then learn what you can use of it and what not.

The 10 most important symbols

The figure's position or poses

The two figures in the image may **not be simply falling, but perhaps flying.** After all, parachuting and jumping off towers are popular pastimes, too!

The Tower – ❶

It is a protection, a watchtower, providing a wide view as well as height, power, and security. On the other hand: an ivory tower, arrogance and isolation, encapsulation, a life of confinement.

Between heaven and earth

We do not see the moment when the figures jumped or were pushed. And also not where and how they land. The image's special energy consists of the condition of flying/falling, i.e. **of existence between heaven and earth.**

The explosion – ❷

At first one thinks that lightning has struck. But the tower with flashes and flames is also a symbol for an orgasm, the epitome of the greatest human energies in sex and in all walks of life.

Drops of gold – ❸

22 drops in the form of the Hebrew J (for fire). A reminder of Whitsuntide (the Holy Ghost in the form of tongues of fire). Golden drops of grace or a destructive firestorm—opposing extremes of energy.

The lightning – ❹

The jagged form suggests a W. *Just as the Magician's* magic wand can stand for an I (myself), the W can stand for we. For good or for ill, the highest forms of life-energy have to do with *others*.

The flames – ❺

Flames of passion. **Negative:** destruction, capriciousness, untamed aggression, call the fire service. **Positive:** to be inflamed with enthusiasm, willingness to help and devote oneself, the divine flame in man.

The tilted crown – ❻

In both a positive and a negative sense: loss of control, opening, both pro-test and con-test fall into insignificance. **Negative:** lack of self-protection, a weak personality. **Positive:** loss of self-importance.

Falling and flying – ❼

Flying is an ancient dream of mankind. And in our dreams, too, flying and falling play important roles. Fear of flying (Erica Jong) can be overcome through positive practice!

The black sky

Negative: loss of horizon, of the overview and of orientation. **Positive:** a light in the darkness. Strength for a new beginning, for the path into the unknown, to illuminate the night. The way to *the Star*.

XVI - THE TOWER

The card warns against delusions of grandeur and a lack of steadfastness. It can come to upheavals, but at the same time there is the (penetrating, yet gentle) encouragement to dispense with one's ivory tower existence when the right time has come!

■ Basic meaning

The *Tower of Babel* is a metaphor for human megalomania. The result is not only the destruction of the tower, but also the Babylonian confusion of tongues: people no longer understand each other. The events of Pentecost represent its reversal: The Holy Ghost descends on the apostles in the form of storm and tongues of fire, and they then begin to speak and each hears the other in his or her own mother tongue. In place of confusion, the raising of barriers of language and misunderstanding.

■ Spiritual experience

Pentecost—the direct communication from heart to heart!

■ As the card for the day

Put in all your energy! And breathe in and out consciously.

■ As a prognosis / tendency

The theme is reducing risks and also the wish to take the plunge and go whole hog. Here the question of the landing is not at issue—only that state of existence between heaven and earth.

■ For love and relationships

The more you can act consciously and directly, the more you will experience love and be protected against aggressive demands.

■ For success and happiness

Live your development as if it were an experiment—keep your eyes open!

The 10 most important symbols

The figure's position or pose

Dedication and contemplation. Perhaps also a reference to Narcissus as he fell in love with his own reflection. Or the figure is seeking her image in vain in the agitated waters.

The jugs

Spiritual capacity, the embodiment of our feelings. Also, ancient writings describe man himself as a vessel fashioned by God, a component of the (water) cycle of life.

Water to water / water to earth – ❶

Here the cosmic cycle is symbolized. **Also:** a place for everything, and everything in its place —some of the energy is used to make the earth fruitful, some flows straight back.

The five streams – ❷

The earth is made fruitful through the water of life. Man as part of Creation and as its active partner. The five streams also stand for the quintessence of each person.

The nudity

Negative: It is a warning against shamelessness and crudeness. **Positive:** personal veracity, a fairytale beauty (in European fairy tales, beauty is generally an allegory for living, genuine verity).

The eight-pointed star – ❸

The eight points of the star are reminiscent of diamonds. The diamond is an ancient **symbol for the pure, true, clear, and purged core of the soul,** the indestructible and inalienable essence that resides in every person.

The foot on the water – ❹

Negative: no access to feelings—one dares not to enter the water, as if the soul were frozen, unable to take the plunge. **Positive:** the water supports, the soul and faith provide a basis and a standpoint.

The tree on the hill

Like the mountain with the peak in the background, the tree with its roots and crown stands for the **connection between heaven and earth,** for the gradual union of the microcosm and macrocosm.

The large bird – ❺

The long beak is indicative of an ibis. The ancient Egyptians worshipped the god Thoth (Greek: Hermes) and represented him with the head of an ibis. An ibis guided Noah after the end of the great flood.

The light blue sky

The heavens = The divine realm and the realm of the will. **Light blue** = (open) sky; (clear) water. **Positive:** lightheartedness, nonchalance, purpose of will, lucid mind. **Negative:** confusion.

XVII - The Star

We use the image of the Star to capture our highest hopes—and also those head-in-the-clouds dreams which have lost touch with reality. A warning against egocentricity and ignoring the rest of the world. It encourages us to find out where we are and what our own contribution to the cosmos may be.

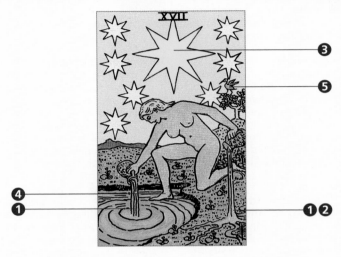

A star is born—and stars don't actually fall from the skies...

■ Basic meaning

All our dreams revolve around this star; one's personal truth is the source of one's dreams. This source cannot run dry—it is simply a matter of finding it and doing as the figure in the picture does: taking it in her hand and letting the earth become fruitful. When the star then illuminates not only the night, but the day as well —then this truth radiates in its full splendor.

Sometimes, though, the card warns against an inappropriate degree of immodesty or exposure.

■ Spiritual experience

Recognizing and accepting one's own place in the cosmos.

■ As the card for the day

Open up, make your contribution! Do away with false modesty and inhibitions so that the full beauty that is you can come into its own.

■ As a prognosis / tendency

Following your own personal star means becoming clear and realizing your own dream. Bad experiences need to be worked through; wonderful hopes dreamt to their conclusion and then brought to fulfillment!

■ For love and relationships

Time for your feelings to thaw out!

■ For success and happiness

Don't hide your light under a bushel—and don't forget that you are only a part of a much bigger Milky Way.

The 10 most important symbols

No figure depicted?

The card warns against the kind of feelings that surface at full moon and threaten to engulf us. We get sucked below, and stand there unable to move or bark at the moon. **Positive:** the gates of heaven are wide, wide open.

Sun and moon – ❶

Full moon, half moon, and sun are merged into one. **Negative:** day and night are one, one lives the whole time as if in a dream. **Positive:** the moon is fully illuminated; the night-time wishes are fulfilled in the day.

Moon face – ❷

Although the moon stands for the vast and oceanic feelings, for the collective subconscious, it has personal traits as well. **In the beginning and at the end we find the personal stories.**

Drops of gold – ❸

15 golden drops in the form of the Hebrew letter J characterize a glittering fluid, the transition between heaven and earth, **the wandering of the souls,** the glowworms, the divine spark.

Dog and wolf – ❹

Dog = tamed; wolf = wild. The path winds through a twilight of animal drives. Ancient instincts and urges handed down through the generations carve out their course from the source to the blue of the mountains.

Crayfish – ❺

The crustacean stands for **age-old feelings and instincts** that make their appearance here—and call to be dealt with and resolved. Or they slip away again, diving down and going back into hiding.

Towers / gates of heaven – ❻

The gates of heaven are open amazingly wide here. Why not simply stride on through? For the towers are a warning against rigidity, against turning into a pillar of salt like Lot's wife in the biblical story.

The long road

The whole path of life; unification of the world and the otherworld; our twin homes in the here and now and in the here-after. A symbol of faith and great dreams that encompass a whole lifespan.

Blue and green stretches

The unconscious and primordial (the crayfish) and the upper reaches of the emotions and beliefs (the blue mountains). Both sides need to be resolved and brought together in the green swards of everyday normality.

The light blue sky

The heavens = The divine realm and the realm of the will. **Light blue =** (open) sky; (clear) water. **Positive:** lightheartedness, nonchalance, purpose of will, lucid mind. **Negative:** confusion.

XVIII - The Moon

The Moon conjures up hidden impulses—even the creature of the depths, i.e. old, deep-seated instincts. A sky decorated with gold seems suddenly to be close enough to touch. This can be upsetting, like a night when the moon is full. An invitation and exhortation to have the courage of your strongest feelings!

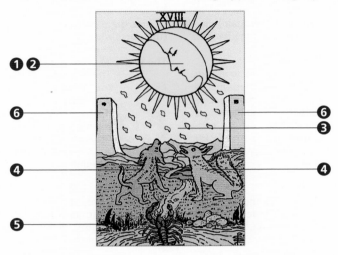

The moon stands for the collective subconscious, for the 'oceanic feelings'.

■ Basic meaning

With this card we often find ourselves in moods that at first we don't understand. There is a danger of being swept away by these spiritual surges. And the great opportunity consists in experiencing empathy with all creatures, feeling at home in all places and in taking on a wider identity. Then we can see what is divine in every event and in every created thing—and within ourselves.

■ Spiritual experience

Empathy, not sympathy! Love, share, but don't identify yourself with other people's emotions.

■ As the card for the day

The greatest feelings and the final matters of life are realities that need to be lived as much as anything else.

■ As a prognosis / tendency

The promise contained in this card is the transformation from a life of longings and cravings to one of release and energetic satisfaction.

■ For love and relationships

Give the nocturnal side of you space (without surrendering to it). Take your partner with you.

■ For success and happiness

Make peace with your God and your world. The card is an encouragement to open one's heart and cast off one's awkwardness.

The 10 most important symbols

The figure's position or pose

The child's attitude expresses abandonment and openness. It is a question of developing maturity (an advanced station in the Major Arcana, i.e., **as an adult to be child-like again**). See how easily it wields the huge banner.

The Sun's face – ❶

Just as *the Moon* stands for the collective unconscious, the *Sun* represents **collective knowledge, conscience and consciousness.** It stands for that center from which we (should) organize our life.

The 21 rays – ❷

The 21 rays show the remaining elements of the Major Arcana, an indication that this card has to do with more than sunny times on the beach, but it is a reminder that *all* of life's positions demand our conscious attention.

The red feather – ❸

The flame of life and the flame of joy (cf. *XIII-Death* and *0-The Fool*). Vitality, potency, liveliness. The red feather shows how truly alive the soul is and reminds us of our essential, inmost being.

The red banner

Looking almost like a great slide, the banner reminds us that we are beings full of vital energy. It is the connecting link between high and low (a similar image can be found in the pole shown in the *six of Swords*).

The gray horse

White = innocence and wisdom. **Gray** = lack of prejudice or something unnoticed, unconscious. Perhaps we remain unaware of the sun behind us and the strength which bears us (the horse).

The wall – ❹

The sun also stands for the world of the Highest and that which is Holy. It sheds its rays in our world, too, and yet this is separate from the realm of the absolute. **Set limits wisely— and keep to them!**

The sunflower – ❺

Does the sun tend to blind us to the dark side of life, make us ignore it, push it away? Or does it rather help us to see what is there? Since the days of Vincent van Gogh, sun and shadow…

Sun and shadow – ❻

…are inextricably linked with the sunflower motif. The shadows speak to us from various parts of the picture: the gray shadow between the flowers and the sun; the shading on the horse. The sun in the background.

The light blue sky

The heavens = The divine realm and the realm of the will. **Light blue** = (open) sky; (clear) water. **Positive:** mirth, lightness, a clear will, a lucid mind. **Negative:** to idolize something or someone; wishful thinking.

XIX - The Sun

The Sun symbolizes daily renewal, light and warmth. Our sunny spot is wherever we can say with full conviction: "This is where it's at!" The way of the sun as well as the way of human consciousness are characterized by creative, multifaceted growth and development.

Every day is a birthday.

■ **Basic meaning**

"Birth is not a momentary event, but a permanent process. Our aim in life is to become completely born…living means being born every minute." (Erich Fromm). We need this permanent state of being born, i.e. self-determined modeling of our lives in a way that is not regulated by habit or routine, but through our own free choice and free will. This means replacing conformist behavior and conventional thinking with a style of life that is truly our own.

■ **Spiritual experience**

"Love God and then do whatever you wish." (St. Augustine).

■ **As the card for the day**

Don't let things get you down. If they get in your way—move them out of the way or find a way around them.

■ **As a prognosis/tendency**

The benefit of age and maturity is that one develops a more open attitude. The sun gives you strength (see banner) and child-like pleasure in your sheer existence.

■ **For love and relationships**

A promising sign for partnership—the more, the merrier—this is possible when it has room to develop and each partner gets his or her fair share of the sun.

■ **For success and happiness**

Be aware of illusion and superficiality and protect yourself against them.

The 10 most important symbols

The Day of Judgment

The bible tells not only of Adam and Eve's expulsion from Paradise, but also of its counterpart: **The return to Paradise on the Day of Judgment. The latter is much less well known, yet it is a firm part of the Christian tradition.**

The figures' position or poses

The figures' gesturing can express farewell or reconciliation. Both of these can be important here: a line is to be drawn under all that has gone before, skeletons in cupboards thrown out.

Trumpet with seven stripes – ❶

The trumpet of the Day of Judgment **awakens sleeping energies and brings the dead back to life.** You, too, can dispose of such powers—or face them, **and:** you will be hearing a great deal.

The orange-red cross – ❷

Like all cross symbols, a sign of differentiation and of connection. The task of taking leave and separating on the one hand and reconciliation and unification on the other.

The angel – ❸

All seven figures in the picture could represent parts of you—including the angel. He stands for **your power of motivation (waking up) and of transformation.** He warns against airy, groundless beliefs.

The six people

This could be a family, a clan, or friends. **Also:** all six figures are a mirror that reflects one's own masculine, feminine and child-like aspects (including the not-so-lovely ones). All this calls for clarification.

The nudity

A warning against shamelessness and crudeness. An encouragement to face up to the naked truth. Openness, honesty, beauty and truth—and not least eroticism and lust.

The open coffins / graves – ❹

No more black boxes. **Negative:** the return of what was suppressed. Certain desires or fears come again and again because they have been neither fulfilled nor resolved. **Positive:** deliverance, frankness, mercy.

The blue-white mountains – ❺

Nirvana or ice age: old wishes and fears find their resolution—the way into a new paradise or mastery over previously unsolved problems. An inspiration to start a process of continual new beginnings and transformation.

The light-blue sky

The heavens = the divine realm and the realm of the will. **Light-blue =** (open) sky; (clear) water. **Positive:** lightheartedness, lightness, purpose of will, lucid mind. **Negative:** naivety, intoxication.

XX - Judgement

We can take the biblical message of the Day of Judgment literally: Today is the Day! Each and every day the task is the same: to wake up and mobilize all our energies. And that means burying what is dead properly—and being open to receive the dawn of what is to come.

The Day of Judgment is today.

■ Basic meaning

You are subject to strong forces, and strong forces are yours to wield. You have the task and the opportunity to resolve and to transform. Basic desires and fears, apportioning blame and blaming oneself need to be worked on again and again until the dungeons of the past have been cleared out and the citadel of the future has a firm foundation. Only then does rebirth bring a new quality of life instead of weary repetition.

■ Spiritual experience

The sense of release after confession, talking things through, a declaration of love…

■ As the card for the day

Draw the line. Go for reconciliation or take the consequences and depart.

■ As a prognosis / tendency

Everything is important. You made decisions in the past and right now you are free to make new ones and choose the path to take.

■ For love and relationships

Learn how to forgive without forgetting—and without hanging on to a grudge.

■ For success and happiness

A break in the daily routine works wonders. Select some guiding principles and visions which suit your experiences and needs—you have huge reserves of energy!

The 10 most important symbols

The figure's position or pose

The figure turns both to-ward and away from the observer: calm and agi-tated, half clothed, half naked. Between alterna-tives, always on the go —**yet going with the flow, serenely balancing contradictions.**

Two wands – ❶

The Magician carries a single wand **(an 'I')**, *The World* two **('I' and 'you')**. With two, the four ele-ments can be brought to-gether (sign of the cross). **Negative:** inconsistencies remain.

The red bands – ❷

The two red ribbons each portray the lemniscate, the sign of infinity. **Posi-tive:** balance, endless-ness, vitality. **Negative:** in a rut, repetition without growth or maturity.

The green wreath – ❸

A crown of laurels and a wreath for a grave. As a wreath it underlines the spatial and temporal lim-its to our existence in this life. The crown of laurels signifies lasting success when we learn how to use this framework.

The ellipse

An ellipse has two fo-cal points (matching the two wands). Sometimes, though, it is necessary to step out of line in order to come to terms with life's inconsistencies!

The mauve shawl – ❹

"Every ascent to great heights takes place on a spiral staircase." (Francis Bacon). **Also:** a symbol for evolution, DNA, an endlessly woven band. Also a sign of personal de-velop-ment.

The four elements / evangelists – ❺

Every person has access to the possibilities of all four elements (cf. *X- Wheel of Fortune*). What he or she makes of them forms the essential fifth element— the quintessence—also to be seen portrayed by the figure in the center.

The (partial) nudity

A warning against lack of culture. Backs up one's will to face the naked truth. Here too: birth, marriage, death—the sa-lient points in the circle of life which are also always associ-ated with nakedness.

Like the legend of Barbarossa

Many legends tell of a princess or giant shut away in the earth, in a mountain, who toss and turn there in anticipation of their release. The card stands for this, too.

The world of the woman

The sum of the digits of XXI = III = *The Empress.* Between them lie 18 steps. 18 = *XVIII-The Moon* = (among others) redemp-tion. Thus *The World* also shows *The Empress,* great Mother Earth, in a state of deliverance!

XXI - THE WORLD

You have two wands at your disposal: It is not only a matter of distinguishing or combining individual opposites, but of those of all four elements. Each person is endowed with all four elements. What you make of them is your personal contribution, your participation in the world!

High time!

■ **Basic meaning**

The green garland: the protection and success which Mother Earth and the world offer us. Then we feel wide and well. This interpretation is comparable with medieval icons, where the whole person is surrounded by an aureola (mandorla), a radiant cloud. However, the garland also represents a limitation, a treadmill which threatens to keep the person fully occupied (walled in) if he or she fails to cast off these restrictions from time to time.

■ **Spiritual experience**

Take part in the world and the world will take notice of you. So you can live two lives at once!

■ **As the card for the day**

Your strong point and your task right now is to step onto center stage.

■ **As a prognosis / tendency**

You develop an awareness for your own limits and opportunities.

■ **For love and relationships**

A woman is shown in the center of *The World*. That means: a man must see himself in the woman to understand the world, and a woman must see herself in the world to understand herself.

■ **For success and happiness**

Don't just ask yourself what you want from the universe. Stop and think what the universe has given you and what it is asking you to do.

The 10 most important symbols

The figure's position or pose

 Open, with his large wings spread wide and chin in the air, ready to take off and launch himself into the air. Keeping one's nose in the air like that can, however, also be a sign of insecurity and arrogance.

Chasm or just a terrace – ❶

 It is impossible to say whether *The Fool's* next step will take him over the edge to disaster, or simply to the next rock. This can help us to concentrate on the moment.

The red feather – ❷

 The flame of life and of joy (cf. *XIII-Death* and *XIX-The Sun*). **Vital strength, potential, vitality.** The red feather shows the liveliness of a person's soul and heart.

The white dog – ❸

 An alert watchdog. Either The Fool himself is awake and aware in the intensity of the moment, or the dog calls a warning and shows what the human next to him has missed.

The blue-white mountains – ❹

 Nirvana or ice age: **As a Fool one is happy and without a care**—in other words, one has already found paradise, or the old, suppressed problems have the upper hand. Take concrete wishes and fears seriously!

The yellow sky

 Radiant sun, but also sensual desire and envy. **Danger:** getting too close to the sun can mean a great fall (mania). **Positive:** illumination and inspiration = strong, reliable consciousness.

The white sun – ❺

 Together with the white rose and white dog. **Negative:** colorlessness, naivety, mind gone blank. **Positive:** nirvana, completion, cleansing, the mind is void (without identifications and attachments), liberty.

The zero point

 The zero warns against a life that turns out to be a waste of time and effort—against unused talents. On the other hand, the origin of a system of coordinates = a reference point for all the rest = the absolute.

The yellow boots – ❻

 Positive: The Fool goes his way with great self-confidence; every step is taken consciously. **Negative:** he seeks his way with his feet instead of using head and heart. What the head has forgotten the feet must fetch.

The bundle on the black staff – ❼

 The burden that each of us has to carry. The black staff stands for one's own activities, at first only dimly perceived. **Task:** to sense and grasp one's potential!

0 / XXII - THE FOOL

The figure of The Fool personifies that openness and indeterminacy which is inherent in every situation—never mind how much it may appear a matter of routine. In this the card stands for the beginning and the end, for naivety or the most sublime fulfillment.

Life is like a box of chocolates…

■ Basic meaning

Zero as an aim and the search for the absolute: inner calm (see the white sun) allows one to dispense with external models and hard-and-fast expectations. Calm and freedom create a great openness. Connections and *synchronicities* come into being between the individual and the whole. One can call it the Forrest Gump principle: just being in the right place at the right time. One cannot achieve and bring about more than that. And less would be to renounce existing possibilities.

■ Spiritual experience

The power of now!

■ As the card for the day

Don't let yourself be driven around the bend. It is foolish to worry about events or consequences which simply cannot be weighed up right now.

■ As a prognosis / tendency

The fulfillment of essential wishes makes you—in a positive sense—happy and devoid of desire.

■ For love and relationships

Two Fools in love are like two *nothings* that link up to make a *lemniscate*—the horizontal eight which stands for infinity.

■ For success and happiness

As a Fool it is your privilege not to know the answers and to learn new things.

The Staves / Wands

The 10 most important symbols

The figure's position or pose

 The legs and arms are spread apart. The hair is mid-length. The figure appears relaxed, ready to act, alert, upright, majestic, neither cramped nor afraid—the queen is aware of her capacities.

The black cat – ❶

 The power of instinct, individuality, unpredictability, a survivor (a cat's nine lives). **Negative:** craftiness, deviousness. Blind spot, stumbling block. You don't let the cat out of the bag.

The sunflowers – ❷

 (In the queen's hand and on the back rest of the throne.) **Positive:** vitality, *joie-de-vivre,* always facing the sun. **Negative:** ignoring the darker side; here: lack of earth, no roots.

The desert with two colors – ❸

 Negative: going astray, being pushed aside, living in one's own little world. **Positive:** creative, transformative power. Working with varying energy patterns. Concentration of forces (pyramids).

The red shoe – ❹

 The left foot/red shoe can be seen under the gown: The unconscious side reacts first. **Red shoe:** devoting one's whole heart and will (from the head to the toes) to a matter. Thoroughness, completeness—and sometimes impulsiveness.

The gray pedestal – ❺

 Positive: neutrality, objectivity, consciousness in movement. **Negative:** indifference, insistence on principle, unyieldingness. All cats are gray in the dark—a warning against unconscious dreams and tenets.

The red lions – ❻

 Passion and strength. Symbol of the true will. Sign of courage, ferocity, sex—but also for unnecessary fears, especially fear of flying as well as being afraid of coming to rest. A warning against showing off.

The throne reaching to the sky

 The task and the capacity to form a link between heaven and earth, i.e. between theory and practice, wish and reality. Note that the back rest is behind the figure and must first be brought to conscious notice.

Yellow and gray

 (robe and desert) **Yellow:** sun, consciousness, alertness. **Also:** envy, deception and delusion. **Gray:** lack of prejudice, objectivity. **Also:** indifference, apathy.

The light blue sky

 Sky/heaven = the kingdom of God (force of destiny) and the realm of the human will (the will of Man is his heaven). The important thing now is to bring fate and one's own will to a happy marriage!

Queen of Staves / Wands

You are like this queen. The card emphasizes your royal dignity and also your feminine attributes! You have and are developing a majestic mastery over the fiery spirits of life. The whole dimension of your humanity with its energy and will to survive is at your disposal—and you need it!

You have the strength to fulfill your tasks!

■ Basic meaning

The mistress of our basic drives: What is my inner motivation? What is it that attracts me? Where can I be as I am?

As is the case with all the court cards, this queen represents an ideal, the perfect mastery over the element in question, here the Wands (fire, drives, deeds, the will). You are like this queen—or you are well on your way! And/or you are destined to meet somebody who personifies this *Queen*.

■ Spiritual experience

Confidence in the creative potential, even when it seems there is nothing there or one has reached the end of the road. Bringing forth new life from what seemed to be a void.

■ As the card for the day

Let the cat out of the bag! Dare to live your enthusiasm!

■ As a prognosis / tendency

This card may refer to major issues: the will to live, creativity, sexuality, survival, career, family, etc. And to your own game of cat and mouse.

■ For love and relationships

Make sure of a good mixture of play, action and adventure. Sharpen up your hunting instinct!

■ For success and happiness

Taken in the right way, opponents and obstacles are really opportunities—even if they mean you have to rethink things.

The 10 most important symbols

The figure's position or pose

A combination of relaxation and concentration. The body is slightly turning, an expression of inner sentiments. On a closer look, the left hand/fist is indicative of his alert readiness—perhaps also of his restlessness.

The salamander – ❶

According to legend the salamander is an animal which can pass through fire without injury. We, too, need not be afraid of trial by fire. In fact, we need such tests in order to find out what we really want!

The salamanders in form of a circle – ❷

The closed circle underlines the motive of rebirth, typically associated with the salamander. Equally, it is a warning against circular arguments and repetition, turning in a circle.

The black lion – ❸

The will, vital strength, and energetic high spirits. However, as both lion and salamander are black and also at the figure's back there is a danger of suppression: once burnt, twice shy.

Red-orange robe/hair (headdress) – ❹

Completely—i.e. from top to bottom—tuned to: fire, will, passion, libido, lust, raring to go (but with a clear mind—yellow/sun)—or, on the other hand, with envy or mania (blinded by the sun).

Yellow mantle with black salamanders – ❺

The mantle with the sun and darkness is a vital factor determining success or failure of projects. The task of coming to terms with light and shadow, maturing through experience.

The green shoes/The green shoulder garment – ❻

The feet show the real steps that we take. The shoulders symbolize our responsibility. Green stands for fruitfulness, growth, naturalness, but also for immaturity, greenhorn.

The crown of flames – ❼

Fired with zeal, great strength of will, on fire for a cause. **Negative:** overheated idealism, overactive intellect. Like this king, we can achieve great things. A great fire calls for a great goal—but a noble one, well-thought out.

The throne extending to the sky

The task and also the capacity to bring heaven and earth together, i.e. theory and practice, wish and reality. But the back rest is behind the figure, must first be accorded conscious consideration.

The light blue sky

The heavens = the divine realm and the realm of the will. **Light blue** = (open) sky; (clear) water. **Positive:** lightheartedness, nonchalance, purpose of will, lucid mind. **Negative:** naivety, wishful thinking, inebriation.

KING OF STAVES / WANDS

You are like this king. The card emphasizes your royal dignity and also your masculine attributes! You have and are developing a majestic, splendid mastery over the fiery spirits of life. Your sovereignty as a human being with your courage, passion, and strength of will are needed.

Actions speak louder than words!

■ **Basic meaning**

The master of the will: "What do I want from life / my partner / to experience right now? How do I want to live?" As is the case with all the court cards, this king represents an ideal, the perfect mastery over the element in question, here the Wands (fire, drives, deeds, the will). You are like this king—or you are well on your way! And/or you are destined to meet somebody who personifies this *king.*

■ **Spiritual experience**

Go through the fire like the salamander and undergo transformation. Experience of a 'trial by fire' and personal catharsis.

■ **As the card for the day**

Go through the blaze to achieve your heart's desire—with skill and without apprehension.

■ **As a prognosis / tendency**

You will be faced with challenges and temptations, unconditional necessities—and limitless self-determination.

■ **For love and relationships**

Independent action and learning to face Death and the Devil unafraid will bring you happiness in love.

■ **For success and happiness**

Scrutinize the motives that determine your actions. The goals must be truly yours so that you can mobilize your greatest powers!

The 10 most important symbols

The figure's position or pose

Rearing up, tempestuous, wild—and yet at second glance also on a tight rein and calculated! The image is of both rider *and* steed. The reddish brown horse is called a sorrel.

Armor, spurs, helmet, gauntlets – ❶

Positive: careful handling of fire and wands brings protection and security. **Negative:** one is fixed in one's ways, inflexible, fleeing to escape or in blind pursuit of something.

Red plumes and sleeves – ❷

A burning will, assertiveness, power, but also pushiness, ruthlessness. **Also:** a burnt child fears the fire. **And:** a bolting horse—someone who can't be restrained.

Yellow tunic – ❸

Sun, light, general consciousness, but also envy, blinding, mania, sensual demands. **Danger:** suppression of the shadowy side. **Positive:** illumination of all aspects = reliable powers of perception.

The salamanders in a circle – ❹

According to legend the salamander is an animal that can pass through fire without injury. The closed circle—**Positive:** reincarnation; **Negative:** circular arguments and repetition, turning in a circle.

The desert – ❺

Emptiness, wildness, wasteland. Heat and fire within us experienced as drought, scorching, overheating. Or a new realm of the will, the apparent nothingness out of which our will can create something new.

With the stave in the desert

Negative: going astray, withering, desertion. **Positive:** overcoming a period of drought, making a garden out of the desert: Confident even in the face of big challenges.

The pyramids I – ❻

Like the pyramids of ancient Egypt, a sign of wisdom and science, mystery and the proximity of the gods. Proceeding according to plan, spiritual activity. **Also:** grave robbers, plunderers.

The pyramids II

Generally a symbol of coming to a point, energy transformation and neutralization. Also peak experiences and high points. Task of raising, lowering, bringing together on a new level.

The light blue sky

The heavens = The divine realm and the realm of the will. **Light blue** = depths of the heavens; (clear) water. **Positive:** lightheartedness, purpose of will, lucid mind. **Negative:** an attack of the blues out of the blue, wishful thinking.

KNIGHT OF STAVES / WANDS

You are like this knight. The card emphasizes your sovereignty and also your masculine attributes! You have and develop a masterful, holistic way of dealing with the fiery spirits of life. You need all your determination as a human being ready to invest a great deal and achieve success.

A hotspur, a hothead—or a benefactor who brings life into the desert.

■ Basic meaning
The master of the aims: "What do I want to achieve? How far am I prepared to go? What is my plan to achieve happiness?" As is the case with all the court cards, this knight represents an ideal, the perfect mastery over the element in question, here the Wands (fire, drives, deeds, the will). You are like this knight—or you are well on your way! And/or you are destined to meet somebody who personifies this *knight*.

■ Spiritual experience
Take up the search. Get through a lean period. Cope, remain true (to yourself), achieve.

■ As the card for the day
Your light is needed where the darkness is deepest. That is where you will find worthwhile tasks that will demand and also develop your full powers. Now is the time!

■ As a prognosis / tendency
You need to act, and the action will show you the right road to take.

■ For love and relationships
Taking on full responsibility and control brings the promise of happiness in matters of love.

■ For success and happiness
Refine your powers of observation and participation. Your intuition and insights will tell you which limits need to be overstepped and which not.

The 10 most important symbols

The figure's position or pose I

Like the page, you look up to the large Wand. The desert and the pyramids, too, are reflections of important aspects of yourself.

The size of the Wand – ❶

The stave is taller than the figure, the impulse larger than the person. A sign of immaturity, but also youth: What points to the future is longer than what has been so far. For those who are young (at heart).

The red plume or flame – ❷

Positive: full of enthusiasm, burning for a cause, prepared to set oneself great goals (three pyramids). **Negative:** misguided zeal/idealism; lack of understanding (feather invisible to figure).

The desert – ❸

Emptiness, wildness, wasteland. Heat and fire within us experienced as drought, scorching, overheating. Or a new realm of the will, the apparent nothingness out of which our will can create something new.

The stave in the desert

Negative: going astray, danger of dying of thirst/withering away, heat, emptiness. **Positive:** overcoming a period of drought, making a garden out of the desert: Confident even in the face of big challenges.

The pyramids I – ❹

A sign of wisdom and science, mystery and the proximity of the gods. Proceeding according to plan, spiritual activity. **Also:** grave robbers, plunderers of the pyramids.

The pyramids II

Generally a symbol of coming to a point, energy transformation and neutralization. Also peak experiences and high points. Task of raising, lowering, bringing together on a new level.

The position of the hands – ❺

Holding with both hands. **Positive:** putting one's hand in, handling (a situation), start, literally grasping something. **Negative:** insecurity, unable to let go, hanging on. **Also:** one thing at a time.

The salamanders in a circle – ❻

According to legend the salamander is an animal that can pass through fire without injury. The closed circle. **Positive:** reincarnation. **Negative:** circular arguments and repetition, walking in a circle.

The light-blue sky

The heavens = The divine realm and the realm of the will. **Light blue** = (open) sky; (clear) water. **Positive:** lightheartedness, lightness, purpose of will, lucid mind. **Negative:** idolizing something or someone, wishful thinking.

Page of Staves / Wands

You are like this page. The card emphasizes your autonomy and also your young and youthful attributes! You develop a masterly, uncomplicated way of dealing with the fiery spirits of life. All your facilities as a human being with a great deal of enthusiasm and get-up-and-go are needed.

Keep hold of what lets you grow!

■ Basic meaning

The adventure of impulses and deeds: "How can I live so that I can really taste life? (So that I don't turn into a fossil?)" As is the case with all the court cards, this page represents an ideal, the perfect mastery over the element in question, here the Wands (fire, drives, deeds, the will). You are like this page—or you are well on your way! And / or you are destined to meet somebody who personifies this *page*.

■ Spiritual experience

Wonder. Develop. Grow. Beyond oneself.

■ As the card for the day

Recall some moments of real happiness and joy in your life. Then, in the light of these memories, decide what you want to do now.

■ As a prognosis / tendency

You will take your leave of mundane, everyday routine. There are fresh energies within you and around you and you are going to let yourself be inspired by them.

■ For love and relationships

The joy of living—*being*—refills your cup of cheer and vigor time and again!

■ For success and happiness

Beware of empty *kicks*, what seem like sources of new energy, but aren't, and which lead you nowhere.

The 10 most important symbols

The card as a mirror

We are like the Wand: engendered by the forces of the earth and the light, a jewel of the life force, offshoot of the past, energy of the present, root of the future. If the shoots are missing—rigidity, dry as a bone, dead.

The Wand I

Wood that feeds the fire. The fire of life that resides within us. Deeds and willpower from the sap of the growing wood. Trial by fire, purging and refining of the will.

The Wand II

Phallic symbol, witch's broom, cudgel, crutch, support. **Also:** growth, aging, ripening, offspring. **Fire:** transformation of mass into energy, of coarse matter into ethereal matter.

The hand emerging from the cloud – ❶

The Wand is a gift to you. You, yourself, are a gift—for yourself and for the world. Accept this gift and make something of it. Grasp it, handle it well, and get your fire burning bright.

The gray sky

Positive: neutral, objective, composed, impartial, without prejudice. **Negative:** unconscious, apathetic, uninterested—instead of on fire rather in a fog and/or a will-o-the-wisp!

The three trees – ❷

Man as a citizen of two worlds (head in the heavens, roots in the earth). Growth, aging, ripening, offspring. Parents and child, self-realization and procreation, independence and community.

River/landscape – ❸

A wide country, great tasks, there is much to be dealt with and achieved. The river stands for continuity in change, for the connection between the source and the outflow. Being and staying energetically 'in the flow'.

Castle/palace – ❹

Home, protection, security, a hearth, clear identification, control over a broad expanse of land, peacekeeping, permanence. **But on the negative side:** closed in, walled in, under control, captivity, aggression.

The 18 green leaves – ❺

Green is the color of nature, vitality, and growth and therefore also of hope. But it can also stand for immaturity, lack of refinement, and things not being thought through properly. The 18 leaves refer back to…

Eight leaves in the air – ❻

…the card *XVIII - The Moon:* life's renewal and emancipation, growing beyond oneself. The eight leaves—falling or flying—underline the transition between heaven and earth (cf. *Eight of Wands*).

ACE OF STAVES / WANDS

A gift of life: the Wand symbolizes your powers of vitality and growth. With these you will undergo constant change, and yet still remain true to your essence—as does the river. And so you will aspire to lofty heights like the castle, radiating your presence into the world, while retaining your links to home.

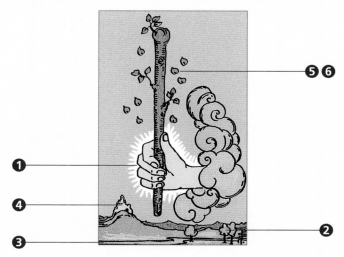

Praise be to that which allows us to grow!

■ Basic meaning

The Wands are the wood that feeds the fire. The sap rising in the staves is an expression of vitality and growth. The message here is of instincts and action, power, success, adventure and everything which makes the blood in our veins pulse quicker. The key term is the will which is forged and tempered in the fire. The Ace provides an elementary way into these forces of fire and the will—they're all yours!

■ Spiritual experience

To go through fire for what one loves. To achieve something for the first time.

■ As the card for the day

Carpe diem!—Seize the day! Get a grasp of what is going on!

■ As a prognosis / tendency

Each card of the Wands is an invitation and a call to do something actively or to let something happen. You will find the answer in the doing.

■ For love and relationships

The will to be oneself and the will to grow beyond one's own frontiers, to be there for others. This is an explosive mixture, but also the fuel of a relationship!

■ For success and happiness

"Speak softly and carry a big stick!"— the method Theodore Roosevelt recommended for reinforcing justified claims. Show who you are and what matters to you!

The 10 most important symbols

The figure's position or pose

 The two staves reflect important energies, drives or flames—contradictions within you or between you and the world. Those that are to be separated from each other and those that are to be reconciled.

The two Wands

 Basic matters in the area of the will and the instincts, e.g., pleasure principle/a sense of duty, profession/family, self-determination/dedication—two people whom one loves, two paths which one can tread…

The globe – ❶

 The ball is in your court! Observe the way things fit together in the world, try to get a grasp. **Warning:** you can't measure everything with the same yardstick. A model only shows part of the truth.

The expanse of water – ❷

 Think global—act local! Oceanic feelings and our connectedness with everything, so that we don't stagnate with a one-sided view of things (only taking one wand into account).

Landscape/large bay – ❸

 On the other hand the available energies have to be used carefully. One needs to know both sides (wands), and yet make a clear decision as to the way forward—setting the ball rolling before time runs out.

The blue mountain – ❹

 Seen as a spiritual landscape, the background shows that everything has its own place—high areas, valleys, near and far. The secret of the marriage of heaven and earth—hope and reality—symbolized by the blue mountain.

The battlements – ❺

 A high vantage point, an overview, control, dominion, calm, equanimity —toward oneself or others as the case may be. To seek, find and take up one's place in the world. Departure—arrival—being.

Cross, lily and rose – ❻

 Show the three classical colors of alchemy: from coarse material (black) via purification / liquefaction (white) to ethereal/ higher energetic material (red). Transformation of energy, the skillful mastery of tasks.

The clothing

 Coordinated tones of red, well orchestrated: mastery of the will, the will to exercise self-control, master of one's own life. **Positive:** one's own taste. **Negative:** one-sidedness, monotony, not much space for others.

The gray sky

Positive: neutral, objective, composed, conscious (corresponding to center position between the two wands). **Negative:** unconscious, apathetic (corresponding to rearmost wand remaining unperceived).

Two of Staves / Wands

Being independent, acting on one's own initiative, creating one's own model, a personal view of the world, being one's own boss. But equally: being a victim of one's own fantasies and ideals, mistaking the model for the reality, arrogance, indecision.

Don't do things by halves!

■ Basic meaning

Two Wands stand for basic energies, important impulses which either complement each other or work against each other. That applies mainly to commonplace intentions, but also to more fundamental interests and larger conflicts. If one forgets to take one of the wands into account, the result is piecemeal. Solving conflicts through patient, gradual work achieves great things.

■ Spiritual experience

"What is my part in the world? What lies within my sphere of influence—and what doesn't?"

■ As the card for the day

Don't get caught between the devil and the deep blue sea. Wait until your decision has matured and then act. Put all your muscle into it.

■ As a prognosis / tendency

Large tasks present you with a challenge. Something new is developing in your current affairs that only you can find out.

■ For love and relationships

With deliberate steps to great goals!

■ For success and happiness

It is possible to achieve great ends. A large stump needs a large ax. Success depends upon your will and your enthusiasm being able to stay the course.

The 10 most important symbols

The figure's position or poses

 This is the only card in which the figure has his back fully turned to the observer. **Positive:** full speed ahead! Eyes front! **Negative:** fleeing toward the front, turning one's back on oneself.

Two shores – ❶

 The wands: the different urges, targets, and wishes that you carry within you. And the opposing shores show where you have come from and where you are going, known lands and unknown, the old world and the new.

The back of the figure – ❷

 Two wands are located behind the figure, who either knows about them or ignores them. **Positive:** you overcome inconsistencies and obstacles. **Negative:** you avoid confrontation with difficult challenges.

The golden sea – ❸

 Insight, gilding, a magic moment, sunny prospects. **But also:** just a reflection, illusion, mirage. Perhaps an easy crossing is possible. But the sea appears like a desert—plans could get buried in the shifting sands!

The ships – ❹

 Sailing ships—do they have anything to do with the figure or not? Did he send them on their voyage? Is the figure about to embark? Waiting to be fetched? Left behind?

The far shore – ❺

 New territory, unknown lands: discovery of oneself, new possibilities. **But also:** distance, aloofness. The central point here is contact with oneself. Does the central figure know himself? What is he searching for? What drives him on?

The 'dirty-yellow' sky I – ❻

 This is the only card in which the sky is depicted as a mixture of yellow and black. These colors stand for sun and darkness, for the polarities of life in general, for the conscious and the unconscious.

The 'dirty-yellow' sky II

 This mixture is an opportunity and a challenge. **Positive:** the resolution of inconsistencies, integration of contradictions. **Negative:** the atmosphere is determined by unresolved contradictions.

Clothing / armor

 The armor reminds one of *IV - The Emperor:* be prepared—or isolated. The robe in red and green stands for heartfelt desires that are fulfilled in fruitfulness and naturalness or in immaturity and naivety.

The headband – ❼

 As with the cards *I - The Magician* and the *Nine of Wands:* being equipped, attentive; all-round awareness ('radar'). Requires viewing everything carefully, including oneself, from the front and the back.

THREE OF STAVES / WANDS

Three of Staves / Wands

How do you see the scene? (1) Someone is about to cross the straits by boat. (2) Or he has arrived too late. The ships have already set sail. (3) Or he observes the proceedings from above. (4) Or he expects or hopes for something. (5) Or he does not know how to go on. (6) Or he has turned away, etc. ...

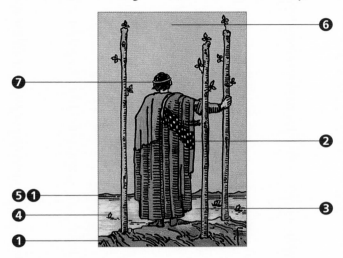

"I must go down to the sea again, to the lonely sea and the sky..." (John Masefield)

■ Basic meaning

An image of entrepreneurial spirit, yearnings, and golden fulfillment. The art of being connected with the world, feeling at home in every port. Two wands are standing behind the figure: a warning against unconscious drives and motives that exercise their influence unnoticed. The face turned away: a warning against fleeing to the front. The solution: to look oneself in the face. Know what one is doing. And why.

■ Spiritual experience

"What's going on there? What has it got to do with me?"

■ As the card for the day

Sort out what you want to achieve, what others are expecting of you, what your actions bring about, what you fail to get done or leave out, who is waiting for you, where you are heading.

■ As a prognosis / tendency

A little patience—you will find a suitable solution that expands your radius of action and your room to maneuver.

■ For love and relationships

Don't wait to be picked up; make the first move! Take time for yourself and what really matters.

■ For success and happiness

Expand your horizons. That will put you and your potential into a new perspective.

The 10 most important symbols

The proportions

The wands are unusually high or the figures unusually small. **Warning:** something is keeping you small, you fall short, you are getting lost in the crowd. **Positive:** high energies, living in a powerful location.

The perspective

The gate and the double lines also mark a threshold. The two figures in the center could be inviting the observer, receiving him/her or bidding farewell. They may be elated or shouting for help.

The two figures in the center – ❶

Some people find that these two, with their attitude and clothing, are reminiscent of the figures in the card *XVI-The Tower.* Both cards have in common that they have to do with very high energetic states.

Blossoms – ❷

This is the only card of the Wands suit that has such blossoms: a flowering will. Either a piece of heaven on earth—highly energetic—high times, or exaggerated expectations, addictive gambling, obsession.

Fruits – ❸

This is the only card in the suit displaying fruits. **Positive:** a fruitful will. Worthwhile goals are set and achieved. **Negative:** the fruits are out of reach of the figures—in the truest sense of the word, the stakes were too high.

The garland – ❹

Positive: a sign of success, enjoyment, fertility (blossoms and fruits). **Negative:** only two wands are connected; part of the energies and impulses remain unused, unfulfilled.

The small group – ❺

Dancers, dance circle, merrymaking—it is not clear exactly what is happening. Perhaps they are traders or vagabonds not allowed into the castle. On the one hand life and liveliness. But maybe too much 'busy-ness'.

The bridge – ❻

Immediately brings the *Five of Cups* to mind. **Here:** the bridging of opposites and conflicting impulses (the Four Wands) which either succeeds and/or is waiting to be accomplished.

The castle

The largest castle in this deck. Security, protection, a safe place, strong sense of identity. **But also:** reticence, foreign dominion. Outside the gates: freedom, joviality. **Also:** no access to one's true greatness.

The figures' faces – ❼

Are almost indistinguishable. The face stands for identity and self-esteem. This may be lacking in the shadow of the castle. The task is to maintain control of things and get the contradictions up and dancing.

Four of Staves / Wands

A highly energetic image. A spirited attitude to living, celebration, the dance of life—full of energy, blossoming, lusty and full of pep. But also: No other card shows the figures as small as this. There is never a greater danger of being sold short or cast as an extra than in this situation.

Celebration or business as usual? Living it up or a tall order?
Welcome or farewell??

■ Basic meaning

The salient features of this card are the proportions. Either the figures are of normal size, in which case the wands must be huge. Or the wands are normal—then the figures must be unusually tiny. And both may be the case at once: festivities and celebration can sweep us up to great heights, or they can bewilder us so much that we hardly know where to find ourselves.

■ Spiritual experience

Go for it! Learn to live with life's inconsistencies and hang on in there!

■ As the card for the day

Your current issues demand a lot of effort. This means putting down more inner roots in order to scale greater heights in your outward life.

■ As a prognosis / tendency

You will recognize when goals are unattainable and expectations too high, so that you can then let them go.

■ For love and relationships

Hot passion and a cool head. The great thing is that each partner has space to grow independently.

■ For success and happiness

Dare to put more vigor in your life and get more from it. That will help you to understand it better. And open up the way to greater successes!

The 10 most important symbols

The figure's position or pose

Object level (see page 9): You see a group, a professional team, family, neighbors. You are involved or you observe the contest. **Subject level:** Five flames burn within you and compete with each other.

Contest / Competition – ❶

Friction, heat, achieving more with teamwork. **But also:** ill-will, pettiness. Aikido, tae-kwon-do, mikado. Carpenters, scaffolders. Building site, workshop, creative chaos, lack of a concept.

Contest / competition II

To ensure that the will remains fresh and alert, our various aspects should wrestle with each other regularly—and we with others. I shouldn't define today what I will want to do tomorrow.

The size of the figures

In contrast to all the other Wand cards, only this one shows adolescents. **Positive:** full of life, in the process of growing. Staying young at heart and/or keeping a youthful will. **Negative:** half-baked, not thought through.

Adolescents I

(Young) men in competition to gain the 'biggest' wand. Playboys, playing children, (addicted) players, the team leader and the spoilsport. **As a metaphor:** competing forces without a clear 'winner' as yet…

Adolescents II

The meeting place of: unconscious and conscious will, active and passive will, one's own will and the will of others, man's will and the will of destiny. This interplay of forces is by no means child's play.

The red figure's hat – ❷

The red hat (cf. *the Page of Wands*, Little Red Riding Hood): Keep it under your hat! **Also:** capped. **Also:** talking through your hat: Understand what you want. Do what's waiting to be done.

Yellow-green ground – ❸

In contrast to the other Wand cards, no desert is visible here. **Positive:** fertility, a place where things can grow, here are nature and vitality. **Negative:** greenhorn, unripe, unfinished.

The colors of the clothes – ❹

The figures' clothes point out the various aspects or colors of the will. Their alternation, their continual process of comparing and testing each other are the quintessential means of forming the will.

The blue sky

The heavens = The divine realm and the realm of the will. **Light blue =** (open) sky; (clear) water. **Positive:** lightheartedness, nonchalance, purpose of will, lucid mind. **Negative:** naivety, wishful thinking, inebriation.

FIVE OF STAVES / WANDS

A game, a competition, trial of strength. The five Wands also form the quintessence of the element fire: our will in its development and progress. Interests and inclinations—between people and within a single person—vie with each other.

The game of life…

■ **Basic meaning**

The card for the game, for the constant interplay which lets the will develop. And the card shows not only the building site of the will, but the will itself in all its finery: as a coming and going, a friction motor, a permanent flow of energy, a source of vitality.

■ **Spiritual experience**

"Man plays only when he is in the truest sense Man, and is only whole as a man when at play." (Friedrich Schiller)

■ **As the card for the day**

Which processes of the will correspond with truly held desires and can therefore really achieve something?

■ **As a prognosis / tendency**

In your private relationships and professional tasks there are new avenues waiting to be explored and played out.

■ **For love and relationships**

Create 'play areas' in your daily routine. It may help to reserve a definite part of the day for them and/or make sure you have your own room.

■ **For success and happiness**

Which acts of the will or strength are a waste of time because they are trying to force things that are no longer needed or not yet due?

The 10 most important symbols

The poses of the depicted figures

The figures show active and passive, conscious and unconscious forces, strengths and weaknesses: You, yourself, in a group or troop. And/or your own powers of self-motivation, the way you lead your life.

The large horseman

Commander, leader, co-ordinator, victor, symbol of conscious will. **Positive:** true will, consistent leadership, good news. **Negative:** pretension, self-delusion, arrogance, snobbery.

The gray horse – ❶

Drives, instinctive action, that which supports and transports the rider, symbol for the unconscious will. **Positive:** vitality, great vital strength and liveliness. **Negative:** animalistic, mindless, at the mercy of blind impulse.

The visible rank and file – ❷

The will to participate, to cooperate or follow willingly. **Positive:** voluntary engagement, active participation, conscious support. **Negative:** dependency, lack of self-reliance, hanger-on.

The invisible rank and file (behind the horse) – ❸

Practically hidden behind the horse, mainly to be guessed at because of the three wands: a rather shadowy will that avoids making decisions and just lets things happen.

The two crowns of laurels – ❹

A wreath of victory and to commemorate the dead. Remember the victims! **But also:** the just deserts. **Your task, your ability:** the art of directing many interests toward a common aim and coordinating their movements.

Ring riding – ❺

The wand and ring signify the ancient sport of ring riding: a fertility cult mimicking the union of the masculine and feminine aspects. **Also:** a wreath on a stave—a symbol for the higher self.

The green caparison – ❻

Here something is in motion which is still very green. **Positive:** great growth potential, nature, freshness, hope. **Negative:** much immaturity, false hopes (idealism), hidden drives (covered horse).

The red and yellow clothing

Red and yellow: heart and sun. **Positive:** lifeblood, will, passion with a cool head, wisdom and enlightenment. **Negative:** lifeblood, will, keenness with envy or mania, suppression of what is dark and of the night.

The blue sky

The heavens = The divine realm and the realm of the will. **Light blue =** (open) sky; (clear) water. **Positive:** lightheartedness, nonchalance, clarity. **Negative:** naivety, wishful thinking, a journey into the blue.

Six of Staves / Wands

United we stand! You succeed in getting the various factors involved to join forces. You formulate your will so plausibly that you are able to mobilize all the forces at your disposal. The result is that you receive support from others and / or can share in the success of others.

Full steam—together we can go through thick and thin!

■ Basic meaning

Not only the rider with the crown of laurels, but also those on foot as well as the horse and the wands are a mirror: for you, yourself, and / or for various people involved in your present situation. Success now depends on good teamwork to coordinate varying interests. You can only gain by paying due respect both to strengths and to weaknesses.

■ Spiritual experience

To take part in a project that is greater than all its individual components. Individual advancement through common progress.

■ As the card for the day

Take on leadership and responsibility. Set yourself worthwhile aims!

■ As a prognosis / tendency

Your present situation provides an opportunity to develop your strengths and your will further. No more half measures!

■ For love and relationships

Come out from your shell: Show yourself with your strengths and your weaknesses—in love and sexuality, too.

■ For success and happiness

When there is only one winner, there are many losers. You will achieve your greatest successes when all/many can share in it! Don't be satisfied with less.

The 10 most important symbols

The pose of the figure

Whether this is just a game or a serious dispute, the wands and the various stages shown in the picture always have something to do with yourself and your development.

The position of the arm – ❷

One thing at a time, concentration on one central task. Possibly a defensive gesture, but also perhaps taking on a wand which is being handed up. Parallel to *I- The Magician:* as above, so below.

The hillock – ❶

Positive: good position, secure stand, superiority, a lookout, overcoming baseness and pettiness. **Negative:** arrogance, haughtiness, disregard of those who are lower than oneself, control complex.

The hillock III

Peak experience, high point, the connection between desire and reality. Together the seven wands can be seen to form a large triangle which is considerably larger than the figure himself.

The hillock II

As the wands generally have something to do with energies (will, drives, deeds, inclinations), there are also varying stages shown in the picture, i.e., different energy and motivation levels.

Two different kinds of footwear – ❸

Boot: protection against being bitten by low creatures—low-mindedness. **Shoe:** civilized life. **Together:** the combination of wild and cultivated aspects. **Positive:** increased liveliness.

The perspective from the bottom up

You have worked your way up. The six wands at the bottom represent the ladder (career) which you have climbed and/or tasks which you have to face and which will raise you to a new energy level.

The colors green and yellow – ❹

Positive: fruitfulness and growth. Justified hope. Freshness. One meets up with (one's own) nature and wildness again. **Negative:** immaturity and envy. Unrest, being under compulsion, false ambition.

The perspective from top to bottom

You go down into the depths. There are stakes to be driven in, fences to be drawn, the project must put down roots. **Also:** getting down off one's high horse, getting to grips with the realities of life.

The blue sky

The heavens = The divine realm and the realm of the will. **Light blue =** the depths of the heavens; (clear) water. **Positive:** lightheartedness, clear will, lucid mind. **Negative:** hit by a bolt from the blue, wishful thinking.

Seven of Staves / Wands

At first sight it appears to be about fighting and dispute. On the other hand, all seven wands could belong to the figure. The card is also an image of achieving a new level—in hecticness, in a struggle (with ourselves or with others)—or by leaving the past behind and planting a new crop.

Is the shoe now on the other foot?

■ Basic meaning

The card for working with energy. When we grasp what is happening we have a chance to *develop*: achieve new heights and delve deeper into the depths. That is an encouragement to let one's personality grow and take one's light out from under the bushel. But when we only grasp what we already hold in our hands and nothing more, the image is a warning against blockages, unnecessary resistance, and being a victim.

■ Spiritual experience

Burn your boats when you have reached the other shore!

■ As the card for the day

Facts can be altered by what you do. The fact of the matter is that you matter—and that's a fact!

■ As a prognosis / tendency

Over-activity and pushiness are of no help at the moment. The important thing is carefully directed, unhurried effort on a new level.

■ For love and relationships

All living things grow, and what grows develops in stages. That is what it's about in love at the moment.

■ For success and happiness

You are on a path of progress. You learn more and more how to cope with bigger tasks and different kinds of energy.

The 10 most important symbols

No depicted figure

One of the few cards without people. **Positive:** growing beyond one's limitations, jumping over your shadow, commitment without the ego. **Negative:** loss of the self, not taking oneself seriously, much ado about nothing.

Perspective I – ❶

The eight wands are coming into land. Something is heading your way. **Or:** the eight wands are taking off like eight spears, lances, arrows. Something wants to get moving, get up and go!

Perspective II

An octave, a scale of energies. **The image of Jacob's Ladder in the Old Testament:** Angels build a ladder for Jacob, allowing him to climb up and down between heaven and earth.

Perspective III

Eight wands that form a fence or barrier blocking the way to the house on the far bank of the river. **But also:** the wings of exaltation, good vibrations. Fasten your seatbelt before taking off!

Perspective IV

The start and the landing are unimportant; the main thing is that the wands are in motion, under way. **Then they mean:** going one's own way, taking on responsibility, don't be a stick-in-the-mud, use your wings.

The alignment of the wands

The coordination of many different tasks, inclinations and interests. You are like a conductor or trainer who is able to line up very varying things. **Negative:** boring regularity, lack of creativity.

The setting – ❷

A wide country, great tasks, there is much to be dealt with and achieved. The river stands for continuity in change, for the connection between the source and the outflow. Being and staying energetically in the flow.

The castle / the house – ❸

Searching for home. On the one hand the house as the aim of one's exertions, or one's efforts are the bridge to reach the goal. **But also:** where you can realize your potential, that is where your home has always been.

The colors yellow and green – ❹

Fruitfulness and growth, but also a warning against immaturity and envy (misguided idealism, nothing but hot air). The eight wands could be a metaphor for our projections (Latin: that which is thrown forward).

The blue sky / the blue river – ❺

Blue: feelings, soul, mind, coolness, yearnings, intensity, naivety. **Positive:** lightheartedness, lightness, clear will, lucid mind. **Negative:** idolizing someone, wishful thinking, inebriation.

EIGHT OF STAVES / WANDS

Much movement; a ladder / scale of simultaneous interests and parallel developments. Also one of the cards without any people on it. One achieves a lot, but loses sight of oneself in the process. Or: one is fully engrossed in one's tasks and builds a bridge between heaven and earth.

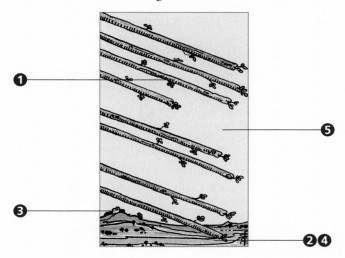

"Stay on the carpet—it has already taken off!" (Johannes Fiebig)

■ Basic meaning

The wands represent vital energies—drives and goals are fuel for the inner fire. *Eight* wands make up a pattern of many energies. This is a card of multifarious energy transfer. Just like interacting magnetic fields, the forces involved can amplify or block each other or cancel each other out.

■ Spiritual experience

To accept one's broken wings and learn how to fly again!

■ As the card for the day

Great tasks require great efforts—in this case more intuition and awareness.

■ As a prognosis / tendency

Reckon with changes on many levels, but also with an increased exchange of energy that makes many things easier and some things possible.

■ For love and relationships

Make sure the energy flow is unhindered and go for good vibrations—within yourself and between yourself and others.

■ For success and happiness

Be or become aware of your own and others' real motivation. Then you will find it possible to combine many forms of energy without the need for any manipulation!

The 10 most important symbols

The figure's position or pose

The task is to cope with a large number of wands (or drives, deeds, desires, targets). **Positive:** you take a step forward, perhaps into unknown lands. **Negative:** Murphy's law—some hungry wolves are waiting for you.

The distribution of the wands I – ❶

The eight wands and the green countryside are behind the figure—probably he doesn't know they are there, hasn't noticed them. Perhaps he has had a feeling that something is afoot, but he doesn't know what it is.

The distribution of the wands II

The positive case is that the figure does know about all nine wands and has deliberately selected one and then taken a step forward. **To be exact:** he has chosen the wand closest to his heart.

The distribution of the wands III

Your task and your ability to come to terms with many different impulses and events—literally to put them in order, and also to learn to accept differing degrees of development (wands of varying heights).

The green countryside – ❷

Green is the color of nature, vitality, growth and therefore also of hope. But on the other hand it can stand for immaturity, lack of finish, 'half baked'. And all of that is behind the figure.

The gray earth

Positive: neutral location removed from prejudice and habit. Equanimity. **Negative:** unconscious action, indeterminacy, apathy, especially in respect to the wands and the green countryside in the background.

The position of the hands – ❸

One thing at a time. Take hold with both hands, handling things, give a hand, hands-on, literally grasp something. **Negative:** insecurity, not letting go, holding on for dear life.

The head bandage – ❹

Negative: bandage, injury, false thinking. **Figurative:** crazy headgear. **Positive:** as in *I- The Magician,* the *Three of Wands.* Prepared, aware, paying attention all round (radar).

The expression – ❺

The way the figure is looking can express intuitive fear or intuitive alertness. **Intuition:** (Latin) the protective gaze, holistic perception. One must see what is happening in order to understand it!

The figure's position or pose II

Possible descriptions: lookout, sportsman, hunter, fighter, on the look out, adventurer, individualist. **Positive:** a very alert, aware person. **Negative:** a ditherer, stay-on-the-fence type, only an observer.

NINE OF STAVES / WANDS

The image of one who is sounding out, perhaps fearfully, perhaps just attentively: There is much growth, change, and transformation. Like a hunter hiding or a scout on the path, you have and can make use of an all-round awareness, increased wakefulness.

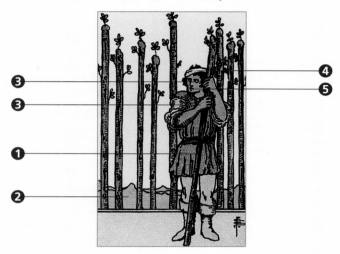

What's going on here?

■ Basic meaning

Wands symbolize fire and urges. The rich green of the countryside is a sign of growth and maturity. The varying lengths of the wands indicate differing degrees of development in a given period of time. Does the figure know about what is happening behind his back? Does he realize what's going on? Has he grasped what is his own?

■ Spiritual experience

Quest for a vision—seek and find your own vision!

■ As the card for the day

Step forward! Quell your fears and fulfill important wishes (for yourself and others)!

■ As a prognosis / tendency

It will do you good to do away with old instincts and suppositions—and accept new impulses and get involved in new experiences.

■ For love and relationships

Cast off the old habits—go beyond your limits!

■ For success and happiness

Have the courage of your own feelings and visions—nothing is more important right now, and this card is the perfect instrument!

The 10 most important symbols

The figure's position or pose

Negative: overburdened, overstrained. **Positive:** when one (literally) follows one's inclinations with one's whole heart, then much can be achieved. Falling forward, giving of one's all, brings satisfaction.

The bundled wands

Your capacity and your task is both to distinguish between many different wands (drives, deeds, energies, interests), as well as to bring them together and unite them: **Lots of wands? No, all the wands!**

The bundled wands II

The ten wands represent a packet of energy, and the person who carries and transports them must also be full of energy! This has to do with a 100% effort!

Wood in front – ❶

Negative: one can't see the wood for the trees. **Positive:** one gets down to the job at hand, concentrates on what's to be done. The drive (the staff, wand) and the intellect (head) grow together.

The inclined pose – ❷

Negative: difficulties in letting go, instead of letting go of the difficulties. **Positive:** a better way to go forward. Striding along, getting ahead, nosing one's way through.

The house I – ❸

The house stands for security, protection, home, wealth, privacy. **And:** identity, a place of one's own. On the one hand, the house is the goal of the efforts that are bringing you closer and closer to it…

The house II

…**and on the other hand:** where we invest all our energies is where our garden grows, where we are already at home even when we are still underway. A sense of home is also an energetic state.

The dirty-yellow earth – ❹

A mixture of sun and darkness, light and shade. **Negative:** mixed motives, unclear or muddy basics. **Positive:** a sense of reality with an awareness for dangers and what is hiding in the shadows.

The red-brown tunic

The same color as the horse in *The Knight of Wands*. In both we are looking at a fox! **Positive:** cleverness of the drives and instincts. **Negative:** wiliness, taking advantage of others. **And:** playing tricks on oneself!

The blue sky

The heavens = The divine realm and the realm of the will. **Light blue =** (open) sky; (clear) water. **Positive:** lightheartedness, spiritual joy, purpose of will, lucid mind. **Negative:** naivety, wishful thinking, inebriation.

Ten of Staves / Wands

A burdened-down figure—a warning against making life unnecessarily diffi-cult for oneself. In a positive sense the picture shows dedication and success: a person who takes on his tasks wholeheartedly, literally pursuing his own incli-nations, getting things done and reaching goals which are larger than himself!

Can't see the forest for the trees, or getting ahead?

■ Basic meaning

The maximum number of wands: the greatest effort, a total effort of will—for the good as well as for the bad. Ei-ther: Completely on the wrong track: abdication of one's own will; wasting energy. Or: acceptance of *all* available vital energies, each and every impulse and aim. The optimal investment of energy. Success. Taking one's life into one's own hands and striding forward.

■ Spiritual experience

Taking up his cross. As a symbol, the cross is older than Christianity, and like the circle or the square, it is a sign for the differentiation between and unification of *all* forces (e.g. of the *four winds*).

■ As the card for the day

Now is the time for you to act. Give all—to attain your heart's desire!

■ As a prognosis / tendency

Only when you give a person or an is-sue your undivided attention will you fully understand him, her or it.

■ For love and relationships

Throw the ballast overboard and get a fresh grip on what is going on and your inner motivation!

■ For success and happiness

Follow your inclination, press for-ward—that will give you a head start.

The Cups

The 10 most important symbols

The figure's position or pose

The Queen regards the precious chalice with appreciation. Her sovereignty is based on this respect for the beauty and value of the cups, the soul, and her needs.

The large cup I – ❶

This is the only card of the Cups which shows this large, sacred, especially valuable chalice. It stands for every person's **spiritual wealth, for the inexpressible worth of his or her soul. And:** a warning against self-importance.

The two angels / elves / fairies – ❷

They underline how valuable the chalice, and their message is: **What is of one's own is holy.** The integrity and the protection of one's individuality is a basic right.

The large cup II

Only on this card is the cup shown closed. The throne, on the other hand, is wide open. Together, they symbolize **the polarity of spiritual existence**. The throne stands for the receptive ear, the cup for one's uniqueness.

The gray throne

The large throne in the shape of a shell is a sign for spiritual openness and participation. **Positive:** encourages patience and an unprejudiced attitude to feelings. **Negative:** a warning against lack of involvement and indifference.

The flowing blue robe

A sign of bonding with the watery worlds. Our bodies are made up of 80 percent water. At home in the water as well as on the land. **Also:** the decisive factor is to be conscious of feelings.

Children / water babies / nymphs – ❸

The inner child, childish/ child-like feelings, good or less-than-good temptations, emotional immaturity, staying young at heart at a ripe age. **The fountain of youth:** experiencing rebirth again and again in this life.

The fish – ❹

Possibly outside the figure's field of vision. **The fish is a symbol of wealth and happiness,** and also overcoming egoistic attitudes (like a fish in the water). This needs to be taken consciously into account!

The cliff – ❺

The triumphs and disasters of life that need to be coped with. It is the repeated experience of these high points and low points that allows us to be born again and again, to grow and thus in the end achieve our potential.

The colored stones – ❻

Soft water moulds the hard stone. **The task:** acceptance of what lies ahead. Stumbling stones which must be cleared out of the way. Making stones skip over the water.

QUEEN OF CUPS

You are like this queen. The card emphasizes your royal dignity and also your feminine attributes! You have and are developing a majestic mastery over the spiritual forces of life. All your skills as a human being with a wealth of feelings and emotional intelligence are needed.

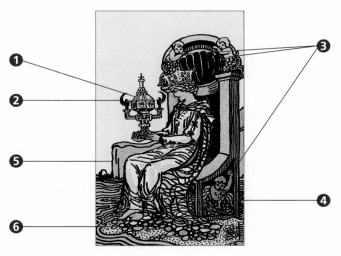

... with an especially valuable chalice!

■ **Basic meaning**

The ruler over the desires of the heart. "What is going to do me good? What do I want for me / us?"

As is the case with all the court cards, this queen represents an ideal, the perfect mastery over the element in question, here the Cups (water, feelings, the soul, beliefs). You are like this queen—or you are well on your way! And / or you are destined to meet somebody who personifies this *queen*.

■ **Spiritual experience**

Trust your inner voice and feelings! Let it flow!

■ **As the card for the day**

Go down to the river, or a lake. Meditate there. Open your heart—for all, not for each.

■ **As a prognosis / tendency**

The pricelessness of the soul: To pay and to receive respect—that is the key to your current questions.

■ **For love and relationships**

The cup is completely closed. And the shell throne is quite open. A hint for you, too, not to go just half-way.

■ **For success and happiness**

You can rely on your gut feelings. The main thing is to learn how to separate the wheat from the chaff in matters of taste and emotion.

The 10 most important symbols

The figure's position or pose

This king is characterized by his open attitude and clear gaze—as well as his remarkable floating stone throne. These are all signs of his dignity, sovereignty, and contentment.

The throne on the water I – ❶

Water supports. **Feelings and belief are the mainstays of this king's existence.** Why doesn't he immediately sink with the heavy stone? Spirit, dignity, awareness—the aerial forces give him buoyancy in the water!

The throne on the water II

Here, not only feelings are at issue, but also personal demands. Longings and desires are concentrated feelings—they, too, hold up the heavy stone throne.

Large gray throne

Gray is the color of neutrality and *sang-froid.* **Positive:** equanimity, lack of prejudice, balance. **Negative:** indifference, here: isolation, (self-induced) loneliness.

The sailing ship – ❷

Positive: ballast is not a handicap, but necessary for a successful voyage = burdens are there to be managed. **Also:** being able to cope with changing winds. **Warning:** danger of being at the mercy of the winds.

The marine animal – ❸

Fish, sea serpent or whatever it may be. What usually stays underwater becomes visible. The king's understanding of inner processes, for feelings and desires, is what gives him his dignity and sovereignty.

The pendant fish – ❹

The task and the ability to express feelings. And speaking out deeply felt needs. **Danger** of hoarseness or breathlessness when feelings cannot find their way into the open.

The cup in the right hand – ❺

Alertness, ability to grasp the needs of the moment, awareness, concentration on the task in hand, treading the path of honesty and integrity. Consciously taking account of wishes and fears is the right way…

The scepter in the left hand – ❻

…which also makes it possible for us to reach many a decision easily. **Awareness means asking:** Which wishes are worthwhile, which aren't? Which fears are worth accepting, which ones aren't?

The primary colors:

red—yellow—blue
Positive: you remain true to your primary aims, and to your original source and motives. **Negative:** your wishes are oversimple. You hardly tap into your greater potential at all.

KING OF CUPS

You are like this king. The card emphasizes your royal dignity and also your masculine attributes! You have and are developing a majestic mastery over the spiritual forces of life. Your sovereignty as a human being with your deep intuition and mighty potential for change are needed.

The yearnings that support us: It bears our weight, holds us up!

■ Basic meaning

The master of spiritual yearnings: "What do I expect of life / of my partner / of this moment? How can I achieve fullfillment?" As is the case with all the court cards, this king represents an ideal, the perfect mastery over the element in question, here the Cups (water, feelings, the soul, beliefs). You are like this king—or you are well on your way! And / or you are destined to meet somebody who personifies this *king.*

■ Spiritual experience

The paths without bounds or banks …

■ As the card for the day

What is the point of a life without yearnings? You have instincts waiting to be sharpened, hunches and temptations that need closer investigation.

■ As a prognosis / tendency

The fulfillment of wishes and working through fears brings us into that desirable state where we are *wishlessly* happy.

■ For love and relationships

Don't worry things like a terrier! It's just not worth your time paying attention to accusations and reproaches—it's much better spent enjoying things to the full!

■ For success and happiness

Find out what those around you and yourself want most of all!

The 10 most important symbols

The figure's position or pose

 A high-profile personality, riding out into the world either to fill the cup or to share its contents with others. Both of these are aspects of a gallant and masterly way with the water element.

The armor – ❶

 The armor with the helmet, spurs, and open visor belong to the attributes of any knight. **Positive:** protection and security. **Negative:** one is fixed in one's ways, a prisoner of one's own 'protective shell'.

The wings of Hermes – ❷

 Attuned to love from top to toe. The link between mind (air) and feelings (water): **dealing mindfully with feelings and beliefs. Warns against:** dogmatism, using one's feelings as an inflexible carapace.

The gray horse – ❸

 Horse and rider together form a unit. Urges and instinct (the horse) play a supporting role. Here, gray is the color of emotional stability. **Positive:** love without fervor and prejudice. **Negative:** inner listlessness.

The gait of the horse – ❹

 Playful, dancing, as during dressage. **Positive:** ennoblement of instincts and drives. Competence in dealing with needs and passions. **Negative:** dressage, subordination, lack of spontaneity.

The Cup in the right hand

 Empty cup: a sign of searching and yearning. **Full cup:** good or not-so-good feelings are carried forth into the world. What the cup contains remains a matter for the observer's imagination.

The river – ❺

 Only by submitting to a process of change can one remain true to oneself. The connection between the source and the outflow. **Allowing feelings to flow and find their channel.**

Mountains

 Negative: obstacles, resistance, formation of feelings. **Positive:** peak experience, high points, tasks for life.

The countryside

 Mountain and valley, meadow and trees—a meandering river: an expression of *joie-de-vivre*, **enjoyment and well-being.** Unspectacular landscape: a pleasant, welcoming atmosphere full of harmony.

The fish – ❻

 Wealth, happiness, multiplicity (fish in a swarm), community, the whole, the totality. Immense feelings, including cruelty, primitive violence. Goldfish or shark?

KNIGHT OF CUPS

You are like this knight. The card emphasizes your sovereignty and also your masculine attributes! You have and are developing a majestic, holistic mastery over the spiritual forces of life. Your devotion as a human being with deep affection and passion are needed.

Spirited from head to toe—or over the top...

■ Basic meaning

The master of beliefs: "What is my belief? What aims are worthwhile? How can I achieve them in the best way possible?" As is the case with all the court cards, this knight represents an ideal, the perfect mastery over the element in question, here the Cups (water, feelings, the soul, beliefs). You are like this knight—or you are well on your way! And / or you are destined to meet somebody who personifies this *knight*.

■ Spiritual experience

Searching for the holy grail!

■ As the card for the day

Avoid gullibility, mistrust, faithlessness or superstition. Test and investigate with wakeful open-mindedness!

■ As a prognosis / tendency

Great passions, life-visions and aims that reach far into the future can generally neither be confirmed nor denied by one's experiences to date. Which makes it all the more important to examine one's beliefs!

■ For love and relationships

Heart and mind are there to help us experience deep and sublime passions.

■ For success and happiness

It is through the mighty emotions that we are most moved—and through which we move most. They are your motor!

The 10 most important symbols

The figure's position or pose I

The page's pose suggests both a positive inclination and reserve, curiosity as well as caution... lighthearted balance as the way toward sovereignty and mastery.

The figure's position or pose II

The position of the legs indicates flexibility, a positive tendency, and reluctance all at the same time. **Positive:** politeness, circumspection, one step at a time. **Negative:** lack of commitment, can't make up one's mind, inconstancy.

Close to the water – ❶

The water is extremely close—the world of the depicted figure consists only of the water and the fish in the cup. And the waters are at his back, perhaps unnoticed by him, in his subconscious.

The fish in the cup I – ❷

The fish is a **symbol for happiness, prosperity, a rich and meaningful life** —but also for coldness, cold-bloodedness, herd instinct (swarm instinct), dependency. The riches of the ocean become tangible.

The fish in the cup II

Obvious: fisherman, angler, diver, marine biologist. **Symbolic:** access to the treasures of the watery worlds: a happy facility in comprehending dreams, premonitions and visions.

The fish in the cup III

Main meaning: access with ease and simplicity, understanding of the riches of the water and the soul. Warning against over eagerness or irresponsibility: The fish is high and dry, taken out of its element.

The clothing – ❸

Man himself is permeated through and through with water. **Tasks:** to recognize one's part in nature's great hydrological cycle. To value oneself as a precious jewel in the stream of life.

The water lilies – ❹

Positive: a sign of beauty, purity and the value of spiritual life. **Negative:** the lilies depicted on the tunic have no roots. Danger of becoming uprooted, getting things out of context.

The colors blue and red – ❺

Positive: spirituality (blue) and will/heart's desire (red) mix and make for high passion. **Negative:** innocent blue eyes and fervor/ego (red) add up and lead to half-heartedness or emotional infringement on others.

The blue headgear – ❻

Spirituality, feelings, beliefs and the mind. **Also:** longing, 'out of the blue', the blues. **Positive:** cheer, lightness, 'keeping a cool head'. **Negative:** wishful thinking, intoxication, too much admiration.

PAGE OF CUPS

PAGE OF CUPS

You are like this page. The card emphasizes your autonomy and also your young and youthful attributes! You have or need a lighthearted way of achieving mastery over feelings or needs. All your facilities as a human being with a great deal of understanding and compassion are needed.

Stick to what helps your soul reach maturity!

■ Basic meaning

The adventure of feelings, yearnings, and believing: "How can I fulfill (my) wishes? How can I reduce (my) fears?" As is the case with all the court cards, this page represents an ideal, the perfect mastery over the element in question, here the Cups (water, feelings, the soul, beliefs). You are like this page—or you are well on your way! And/or you are destined to meet somebody who personifies this *page*.

■ Spiritual experience

Successful wishing...

■ As the card for the day

Express your wishes and fears clearly and directly. And act accordingly.

■ As a prognosis / tendency

New insights. With empathy, meditation and understanding you can recognize your own path—that way you can be a help to yourself and to others.

■ For love and relationships

Take your heart by the hand and stand by your desires and demands!

■ For success and happiness

Don't let the fish dry out! Speak out what your heart wants to say!

The 10 most important symbols

The card as a mirror

Water is a symbol for spiritual life. The cups give the water (as a representative of our spiritual aspects) form and being: needs, dreams, premonitions, wishes. Man as a vessel: participation in the flow of life.

The Cup I – ❶

Whether in the tarot or in the interpretation of dreams, in fairy stories or in astrology: **water always has to do with the soul, spiritual life, feelings, beliefs.** The link between water and the mind/spirit points to spirituality.

The Cup II

The cup stands for what makes water (feeling, belief) tangible—i.e., our spiritual needs, wishes, and fears visible to the inner eye. Double meaning: positive and negative feelings must be separated from each other.

The five jets of water I – ❷

The Cup is the source of five streams of water. **Or:** five jets rise up to the Cup. An image of the great natural cycles and a symbol for the way individual people are connected with the River of Life.

The five jets of water II

The link between ocean and Cup: connection with everything else like a drop of water in the ocean. **The individual jets:** differentiating between oneself and all others; sorting and distinguishing different feelings.

26 drops – ❸

Divine grace. Human tears. **Connection between water and air:** spirituality. Highlights the transition between above and below. 26 letters, the language of feelings.

The white dove – ❹

The Holy Ghost, the divine. Also, the dove of peace, symbol of wisdom (Sophia) and love (Eros, Aphrodite). **But also:** mental hysteria (Hitchcock's *The Birds*).

The cross/the letter – ❺

The letter could be a W and refer to the deck's author, A. E. Waite. And/or it is a reference, together with the eucharistic host in the dove's beak, to the Church's role as bringer of the creed.

Water lily/lotus – ❻

Beauty, purity, enlightenment. East Asian traditions, and especially Buddhist symbolism, make a metaphor out of the way the lotus emerges from a swamp to produce an unusually beautiful bloom.

The hand emerging from a cloud

The Cup is a gift to you. You, yourself, are a gift—for yourself and for the world. Accept this gift and make something of it. Listen to the language of your feelings.

ACE OF CUPS

*The gift of life: The Cup symbolizes the individual spiritual life of a person, the
capacity of a soul, its wishes, fears and all feelings. The great waters stand for
the sea, for the oceanic feelings, for our connectedness with everything.*

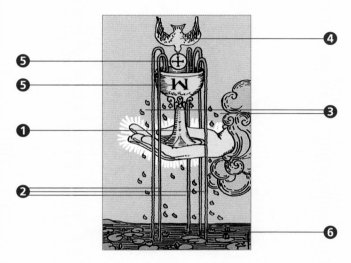

Praise be to what makes us feel and flow!

■ Basic meaning

The Cups are the vessels that give our
feelings a home: This has to do with
spiritual needs, longings, belief, and
everything that moves us and (ful-)
fills us inwardly. The essential thing is
flow. The key notion is the soul, which
is purified and purged with water. The
ace provides an elementary way in. It's
all yours!

■ Spiritual experience

Baptism. Transformation and the
start in a new life.

■ As the card for the day

Cleanse away what is muddying your
feelings. Clarify your emotions.

■ As a prognosis / tendency

Each Cup card represents an invitation to receive something (passive)
or let something go (active). When
things flow you will find the answer
you are looking for.

■ For love and relationships

We are as the ocean and the Cup—in
contact with all things, and yet free
and independent. These contrasting
aspects provide for tension and release in your relationships, too.

■ For success and happiness

This is not the time for big promises
or pledges, but for personal integrity.

The 10 most important symbols

The figure's position or poses

The figures are almost in half-profile. **Positive:** two halves make a whole. **Negative:** if one always sees the other person as one's better half, then one is reduced to being only half a person, love only half-hearted.

The winged lion's head I – ❶

Mighty emotions. In a positive sense this is a protective shield which lends wings and releases a huge amount of energy. Strong energies (of the heart and of a sexual nature) reinforce each other and create an inspiring energy field.

The winged lion's head II

Emotions that have not been grasped, or a spell. Locked together, unable to move from the spot. A double bond, in each other's clutches, wishes and fears intertwined.

The staff of Hermes – ❷

Stands for the link between drive and intellect. The snakes coiled around it make larger and larger coils the higher they are. In order to put a stop to this development, one must go back to the roots.

Laurels and crowns of blossoms – ❸

Looking at the **negative aspect,** this is the start of an entangled relationship. **Positive:** how love and being loved can turn daily routine into a celebration and raise ourselves onto a higher plane.

The High Priestess's colors – ❹

White and blue represent the feminine side. If this aspect remains obscure, underdeveloped, or half-hearted, then they also stand for the *anima-I* part of our spiritual life: fearful, demanding, disorientated.

The Fool's colors – ❺

Black and yellow represent the masculine aspect. If this aspect remains obscure, underdeveloped or half-hearted, then they also stand for the *animus* part of our spiritual life: idealistic, selfless, obsessed.

The house on the hill

The hills in the image stand for the ups and downs of life. **Task:** we should look for our better half within ourselves and thus open the way for a real partnership. That way, we automatically find our way home.

The red shoes – ❻

Lifeblood, emotions, passion. **Positive:** vivacity! **Negative:** the spellbound or jinxed aspect of our emotions, which is sometimes only indicated by small details.

The light blue sky

The heavens = The divine realm and the realm of the will. **Light blue =** (open) sky; (clear) water. **Positive:** lightheartedness, spiritual joy, purpose of will, lucid mind. **Negative:** being over-admiring, wishful thinking.

TWO OF CUPS

TWO OF CUPS

Two Cups emphasize the polarity of our spiritual life—sympathy and antipathy, desires and fears, affection and rejection. Each of us must find a way of recognizing and then coping with the internal conflicts within our souls.

The red lion—a huge emotional resource, both for good and for ill!

■ Basic meaning

Two Cups stand for basic energies, important feelings which may be in conflict with each other or complementary. That has to do rather with normal everyday intentions. But it also applies to fundamental interests and larger conflicts. The staff of Hermes and the winged lion's head can mean the felicitous bond as well as the unhappy entanglement of two souls.

■ Spiritual experience

The first great love…

■ As the card for the day

Dealing successfully with strong emotions—a lifetime's task that we have to tackle anew time after time.

■ As a prognosis / tendency

Consciously taking account of feelings and needs is always the decisive factor.

■ For love and relationships

Let your soul spread its wings…by doing something for yourself or in company, talking things over, letting go, a reconciliation.

■ For success and happiness

Shared joy is redoubled joy. Shared sorrow is only half as bad.

The 10 most important symbols

The figure's position or poses

Positive: a round dance, a common experience which lends wings to the heart and opens horizons. **Negative:** none of the cup bearers appears very open, nor do they address each other (or the observer) directly.

The figure's position or poses II

Here, in both positive and negative senses, we see **'women power'** in action, a primeval image recalling the Great Mother, the three Graces, the three Moirae, the Great Goddess as virgin, mother, and wise woman.

The pose of the depicted figures III

The figures are in movement and also they regard each other from a somewhat oblique perspective. This is a representation of the power of **the emotions** (Latin: movement, expression).

Fruits / harvest – ❶

The harvest is rich—i.e., rich grounds for celebration. Enjoy life in community—you belong. **Task:** Don't forget to be thankful for all that has been given to you.

Raising the Cups I – ❷

Positive: group experience, raise high the cups, party, the fruitfulness of the soul in its ability to rise above itself. **Negative:** nose in the air, emotional arrogance. Putting on a show.

Raising the Cups II

As is the case with the *Nine of Cups* and the *Ten of Cups:* We see the theme of the raised Cups here, too…

On tiptoe – ❸

Positive: dance, liveliness, lightheartedness, raising the cup, giving a toast. **Negative:** façade, artificiality, pretension.

The dance – ❹

Negative: group pressure, inebriation, losing oneself. **Positive:** life is a festival, "Just say the magic word, and the world begins to sing." (J. von Eichendorff)

Red, beige, white – ❺

The figures also stand for the unity of body, mind, and soul. Red is for the soul, white for the mind and beige for the body. **Positive:** love with all your senses! **Negative:** division between physical, mental, and spiritual love.

The light-blue sky

The heavens = The divine realm and the realm of the will. **Light-blue =** (open) sky; (clear) water. **Positive:** lightheartedness, spiritual joy, purpose of will, lucid mind. **Negative:** naivety, wishful thinking, inebriation.

THREE OF CUPS

A fruitful spiritual life involves exchange of ideas, togetherness but also independence within a group. And, too, the trinity of body, mind and soul in an individual. The card's positive message is of the magic of feelings—and its warning is against spiritual arrogance!

The best things in life are three!

■ Basic meaning

This card highlights a great opportunity, which at the same time can be a great danger—that boundaries between people become indistinct. It is not easy to see which figure is holding which cup, what each one is actually doing. Action and reaction, original and echo are mixed up together. In a good sense: the remarkable ability of the soul to grow and become like others. Negative: a 'we' feeling which swallows up the individual.

■ Spiritual experience

A great celebration. Making a fiesta of the daily round!

■ As the card for the day

Don't be afraid of emotional reactions. Open up to others or make your limits plain (and don't be surprised if you need a little practice).

■ As a prognosis / tendency

Life becomes a festival when a host of feelings bring forth fruit together!

■ For love and relationships

A well-timed word can do miracles. Say what you think—go on, it's worth it!

■ For success and happiness

A favorable card when we see it as a sign of emotional intelligence. The emotions that we are aware of are the rewarding ones.

The 10 most important symbols

The figure's position or pose

This could be you or somebody else: either simply withdrawn, or sulking—or perhaps meditating, turning things over in their mind. Waiting for something, or giving the creative forces a chance to power up.

The tree – ❶

From time immemorial, **a sign of vitality and fruitfulness.** Also, the tree can stand for mankind: with his roots in the earth and crown in the heavens, man inhabits two different worlds at the same time.

Root, trunk, and crown I

The figure's position close to the tree's roots can be symbolic of his connection with his own roots. In this sense the card portrays positive withdrawal, for phases of coming to rest, dreaming, meditating.

Root, trunk, and crown II

In other cases the card can be understood as a reminder that it's time to get up and reach for the sky like a tree. A time to stand up straight and present oneself to the world in full leaf and beauty.

The hillock – ❷

The figure is a little raised. Sometimes it's good to put a distance between oneself and certain experiences and issues so as to process and perhaps compensate them—that's how insights and inspiration are born.

The fourth Cup – ❸

Spiritual growth, inspiration, a new Cup, a new beginning, a new area of experience opens up. Nevertheless, this is also about departure and rejection: "May this cup pass from me, if it be thy will!"

The hand extending from the cloud – ❹

It is the hand of Fate, or of God, which proffers the new Cup. Or, on the other hand, a figment of the imagination, a self-made ghost come to haunt our private thoughts.

The color light blue

A wide-open sky above you. Light blue stands for water as well as air. The mixture of water and air, though, is the spirit, spirituality. What lends our soul its wings…

The cloud – ❺

…albeit also vague desires or unfounded fears. The cloud, too, consists of water and air. The grayer it is, the less transparent —and the more there is that needs clarification and filtering.

The color green – ❻

warns against personal immaturity (a "greenhorn"). And it also encourages thoughts of vitality and further growth, especially in respect to dealing responsibly with one's own experiences and needs.

FOUR OF CUPS

A new spiritual experience is in the offing (the Cup from the cloud).
Sometimes you should accept the cup, for good or ill—whether it contains
sweet wine or bitter medicine. Another time it is right to reject the cup and
demand: "Let this cup pass from me!"

Back to the roots!

■ Basic meaning

The depicted tree is both a symbol of nature and of mankind as a special part of nature. While the figure is sitting next to the tree's roots, this is an expression of his having gone back to his own. On one occasion it may be a hint to take a break from the daily routine in order to find time for reflection and contemplation. But sometimes it is time to put a stop to a period of brooding and reorientation and, like the tree, stretch up into the sky.

■ Spiritual experience

Experience grace and thankfulness! Draw strength from an experience of nature, talk to a tree!

■ As the card for the day

Take a good look at your feelings. Take a break. Then draw clear conclusions. But don't rush yourself.

■ As a prognosis/tendency

Meditation helps you find the words to describe experiences and impressions which have failed you till now.

■ For love and relationships

He who wants to reach for the sky must first delve deep within himself! And that applies to the ups and downs in love, too.

■ For success and happiness

Sometimes you only have personal reasons for doing something. And those are more than good enough to lead you along the path toward happiness!

The 10 most important symbols

The figure's position or pose

Black is the color of grief, but also of the unknown, the unfamiliar. Who is the depicted person? Could it be you? Someone close to you? This is also where we experience the black night of the soul!

The black figure I

Sometimes one feels empty like the overturned cups, and burned out; often, the only way out is to accept one's sadness, give one's feelings free rein, and let the tears flow.

The black figure II

But often enough the black figure has nothing to do with grieving or burn out. In a positive sense he is also a symbol of transition. When something truly new begins in life, we first have to go through a tunnel.

The black figure III

When something comes in sight that is completely new to us, quite beyond our previous experience, then our soul—the inner voice—says: "Darkness—no idea!" It is still dark, like an unexposed film.

The overturned Cups – ❶

They stand for **past experiences of the heart** (red) which need to be grieved over or let go. Learn to forgive without forgetting and learn to remember without getting stuck in the past.

The standing Cups – ❷

Something is past, has flowed on—but something new is waiting for you as well. New cups, new capacities for your wishes and fears! **New spiritual possibilities and truths.** Turn around and address them!

The river – ❸

Only he who remains in a state of change remains true to himself. The river is an old symbol for continuity and reliability on the one hand—and continuous flow, constant change on the other. At one and the same time!

The bridge – ❹

Have faith in the future. Go across the bridge, then what is new is no longer unfamiliar. Like the figure in the image, you can turn to the new. That is the way through the tunnel—across the bridge.

The view of the back – ❺

The back is the region of shadows, of the unseen and therefore of the unconscious. But there is also a **warning:** don't turn away from yourself. Come to terms with yourself and those around you.

The (ruined?) castle – ❻

As a ruin, this building shows the march of time like the overturned cups. If you see it as an intact castle, then it can be one's goal, protection, and home—to be reached by crossing the bridge.

FIVE OF CUPS

On the one hand: Sadness, anxiety, spiritual exhaustion. Or again, the card can stand for a successful start on something really new, something that you only had a vague idea about before. It takes courage and determination to find your way out of the tunnel.

The quintessence of the Cups: flow and permanent change.

■ Basic meaning

The bridge to a new shore is there. The challenge is to step onto new territory, and that means crossing a bridge. We encounter the *shadow*. In a psychological sense the shadow is a kind of doppelganger, the *alter ego*. The black figure also represents this shadow theme. The shadowy figure personifies one's own unlived aspects, wishes, and fears that have so far remained in the subconscious.

■ Spiritual experience

A metamorphosis—a period of transformation, one of life's tunnels, the start of a new phase in life.

■ As the card for the day

Don't run away from (your) feelings. You have been waiting for this new beginning for a long time.

■ As a prognosis / tendency

Two cups are standing. You can choose which feelings and needs you take with you—and which ones you leave behind.

■ For love and relationships

This card brings out sadness, anger, ill will, resentment and other emotions if they have been kept in the background up to now. Now is the time to sort out disputes which are waiting to be resolved!

■ For success and happiness

Disillusionment: recognizing an illusion, learning a new lesson, sets a huge amount of energy free.

The 10 most important symbols

The poses of the depicted figures

You could be one of or all three of the figures here. There may be a reference to your attitude toward childhood and to children. How you deal with illusion and the truth, what you make of a rich store of past experiences.

Cups with flowers

This is the only card which shows a cup with flowers in them. So the theme of the card is a blooming spiritual existence. And for this we return to the realms of childhood and/or the adventure of youth.

Children / Dwarves

The large dwarf and the little woman depict ourselves. It is a sign of spiritual maturity when as adults we succeed in being children again! And that means taking another look at the experiences which we had in childhood.

The little woman facing forward – ❶

Those who, at first glance, see the forward facing version of her face first and foremost see and seek a "Yes," i.e. agreement in relationships and matters of feeling. They find it more difficult to say "No".

The little woman facing away – ❷

Those who, at first glance, see the face which is looking away tend more towards a "No," in other words: setting limits in relationships and matters of feeling. For them, it is saying "Yes" that they find more difficult.

The little woman's double face

The reference is to an ancient trick image: at the front a young woman, at the back old hag—or the young woman in front and death at the back. The old name for the image, dating from the Middle Ages, is Vanitas (emptiness, vanity).

The 'X' cross – ❸

This cross is not just for decoration. As adults, we can reset the points. We return to our childhood in order to investigate the double-facedness of our experience, to dig up the missing aspects.

The thorn-apple blossoms – ❹

The thorn-apple is a member of the nightshade family and known as a witch's herb. It can be either a poison or a medicine, depending on the dosage—and one's knowledge. The same applies to our spiritual origins.

The watchman with lance / wanderer with staff – ❺

The wanderer underlines the aspect of change, the watchman that of protection—but also for control or childhood experiences. Sometimes it is not easy to access old memories.

The white glove – ❻

Elegance. Caution, gentility. And: a person who doesn't want to get their fingers dirty. Possibly a fear of some truths about one's own childhood and origins.

SIX OF CUPS

What does one need to allow one's spiritual life to blossom out? The card makes it clear: The adult can—and must—become a child again. And that also means resolving those bad childhood experiences and returning to a child-like openness and joy.

An image of interaction with others—and one's relationship to oneself!

■ Basic meaning

A double face: the small woman looks away from the manikin/dwarf (the yellow patch is her face, with an orange-red scarf on the left and right). And she is also looking toward him (now the yellow is her hair, with her face to the left, and the scarf to the right). Both of these points of view belong to the image. Most people spontaneously only see one of the variants. But we need both: setting limits and establishing contact, No and Yes!

■ Spiritual experience

Falling in love, completing a therapy, bathing in the fountain of youth!

■ As the card for the day

A sheltered space in which one can show one's vulnerability. Dare to take a look at your emotional experiences, but don't demand too much of yourself.

■ As a prognosis / tendency

You expand the horizons of your understanding. Today, you have *more alternatives* at your disposal than you did as a child.

■ For love and relationships

Do away with childish patterns of reaction and do what you, as an adult, have long since wanted to do!

■ For success and happiness

Take this opportunity as it presents itself to cast off old fears and fulfill important wishes.

The 10 most important symbols

The black figure

If you look closely, you can see yourself in the dark figure—but equally in all of the forms to be found in the seven cups. Your task is to distinguish between worthwhile and worthless desires.

The black figure II

Positive: coming to terms with the shadows of the past in order to be able to reach one's goals. **Negative:** putting one's head in the clouds so as to ignore the here and now; to become a shadow of one's true self.

The realm of clouds

To recognize and claim one's personal assets. The opposite side of the coin consists of greed and dissatisfaction. The trick is to affirm what is one's own, and not to deny oneself in favor of illusory ideals.

The curly-haired head – ❶

A symbol of beauty and eternal youth, a warning against vanity and narcissism. The head invites one to face oneself and accept oneself as one is.

Castle / tower – ❷

Castle—Positive: protection, home, security, safe and sound. **Negative:** repression, isolation, or arrogance. **Tower—Positive:** an overview, alertness. **Negative:** ivory tower, out of touch with reality.

Treasure / Jewelry – ❸

Inner and outer riches. The true values, personal brilliance, and worth. **In a negative sense:** filthy lucre, money as compensation for inadequacy, insecurity in respect of one's own personal value.

Crown of laurels – ❹

The crown of laurels can be both a sign of victory and of death. This cup also bears the image of a skull (see also the cards *XXI-The World* and the *Six of Wands*). **Task:** to render one's own life useful.

The dragon – ❺

In European legend a fearsome monster (St. George, the dragon slayer). In Chinese tradition it can also be a bringer of luck. **You, too, possess extraordinary powers.**

Snake – ❻

Low, sly patterns of behavior and instincts—the one who crawls in the dust. And equally, a symbol of wisdom, transformation (sloughing off old skin), and higher development (the upwardly striped snake).

The shrouded figure – ❼

The enigma and mystery which resides in every person. This precious and wonderful trait is already visible in you, but it will only come to full fruition if you pursue your personal development.

Seven of Cups

Fantastic possibilities open up in front of you. Choose what you will—cast off the shadows of the past and seize what is yours to take. Or: in your fertile imagination you live in a world of wonders, while the real you leads a life in the shadows. Desire and reality are like day and night!

Here, nothing is obvious!

■ Basic meaning

Everything has two meanings, like the castle that stands for power and greatness, but also isolation and loneliness. Here you are invited to take a look behind the scenes, to order your wishes and anxieties with a cool head—for unfulfilled wishes can lead you astray just as well as ones that are fulfilled, but turn out to be illusory or just superstition. The solution: evaluate your experiences, grow into spiritual maturity. Draw your limits, achieve your aims, find out what does you good.

■ Spiritual experience

Learn to differentiate, don't get lost in your own smoke screen!

■ As the card for the day

Separate the wheat from the chaff. Get to know your wishes and fears better.

■ As a prognosis / tendency

"Qui vivra verra": He who shall live, shall see. The proof of the pudding is in the eating.

■ For love and relationships

Investigate your experiences thoroughly and pursue those desires that radiate the greatest energy.

■ For success and happiness

Your wishes should serve you and your happiness, and not the other way around! The aim of wish fulfillment is to be happy without any more wishes …

The 10 most important symbols

The figure's position or pose

Who is underway here? Is it you, your partner, a stranger? Are you following your inner flow, or have you turned your back on yourself—running away from yourself?

The Moon and Sun

The sun and the moon fight for mastery—or they complement each other. The sun usually stands for the conscious will. The moon represents what is one's own, private, below the level of consciousness.

The river – ❶

The river can be seen in different ways: It may seem that the red-robed figure is walking with the flow, i.e., toward the mouth. Or upstream, along the river toward its source.

The red robe – ❷

You will find a way if you rely on and follow the power of the soul and the strength of your wishes (moon and river) and proceed with strength of will and passion (the color red) and awareness (the sun).

The mountain – ❸

Mountains can stand for difficulties and blockages, but equally for peak performance and summit experiences. A psychological axiom: if you want to achieve great things, you must follow the flow of your spiritual energy.

The ravine – ❹

You master obstacles and cope while under pressure when, like water, you follow the lay of the land—in other words, you go to where the greatest energy is to be found and then do what that energy helps you do best.

The mouth/source

The path to the wellspring takes you back to your roots, a necessity at every stage in life. The path to the river's mouth is that of your calling and destiny, what you have found to be right for your life.

The view of the back

Positive: you also take account of the other side of the coin, pros and cons of a person, a situation, and also of yourself. **Negative:** you harp on to yourself about your own disabilities (weaknesses, handicaps).

The staff – ❺

It is reminiscent of the cards *IX-The Hermit, VII-The Chariot* and of the wanderer in the image of the *Six of Cups*. It stands for confidence in ones own strength and for being conscious of one's own weak points.

The gap between the Cups – ❻

The cups take you into their midst. No longer do *you* have the cups in your hand, but *they* have you! You capacities are insufficient for dealing consciously with mighty feelings.

Eight of Cups

Dreams and visions which are not immediately obvious make up a valuable part of your feelings. Let them help your consciousness and your powers of discrimination grow. Start searching. But be aware of the card's warning about the kind of restlessness hat strides on too hastily, missing the very goal (the Cups).

Go wherever your heart takes you!

■ **Basic meaning**

A parable for life's journey: each of us carries a river within himself/herself. We say that everything flows, but sometimes the inner stream is just a trickle—and sometimes it is a flood that inundates everything. Your task is to open up to your inner flow and to *exercise an influence on it.* That is the best way to deal with obsession and overwrought enthusiasm as well as lethargy and loneliness.

■ **Spiritual experience**

Understanding one's own destiny. It is all the easier to make out, the closer we are to our flow.

■ **As the card for the day**

"The mills of God grind slowly, yet they grind exceeding small." That means patience can help, and there is a time for everything.

■ **As a prognosis / tendency**

There is a time for everything. And everything is important.

■ **For love and relationships**

Encourage yourself and your partner to go each his or her own way. Very good for love!

■ **For success and happiness**

Go with the flow. Following the flow of energy not only takes the least effort, but it also achieves the best results!

The 10 most important symbols

The figure's position or pose

In this image you can see yourself—or somebody you know—who in some ways is very open, in other ways very clammed up. As observer, you can see the large array of cups—but has the depicted figure noticed them?

Red hat/red stockings – ❶

Will and passion, love or jealousy find their expression in the color red. Also, we see the blue of the soul and spirituality as well as yellow, which can stand for sun and light, but also envy.

The Cups at the rear

The spiritual riches indicated by the nine cups are entirely outside the figure's field of view. It may be that this expanse of feelings, needs, and wishes makes itself felt on an unconscious level—behind his back.

The folded arms – ❷

Positive: a sign of anticipation, preparedness, and patience (the forearms and hands form a horizontal figure of eight). **Negative:** laziness, a mere onlooker who doesn't get involved, hasn't grasped what's going on.

The spread legs – ❸

The position of the arms and legs reveal conscious and unconscious attitudes: The lap is open. This is a sign of openness, of demands and expectations in respect of drives and instincts.

The white robe – ❹

White stands for beginnings and/or for completion, for naivety and colorlessness, but also for maturity and wisdom. Like the word wisdom and like white light, both signs of accomplishment and wholeness.

The Cups in a row – ❺

Positive: you have the ability to grasp a complete entity or collection and provide for order (networks, larger groups, a range of needs). **Negative:** you don't find it easy to 'step out of line' from time to time.

The somewhat raised Cups I

A question of perspective: One can regard the semicircle of cups as if they are **behind** the figure. They can also be seen as if they are arching **above** the figure…

The somewhat raised Cups II

…(thus providing an introduction to the raised cups that we find in the *Ten of Cups)*. Their raised position symbolizes **lifting/raising** in all senses of the words:…

The somewhat raised Cups III

…**uplifting:** positive and elevating experiences and feelings. **Bringing something to an end,** e.g., raising a siege. Finally, raising something or oneself onto a higher level, i.e., dealing **more successfully** with the cups.

NINE OF CUPS

Now we have to do not with just one, two, or three cups, but a large collection of them—feelings, longings and beliefs. Your whole emotional 'household' comes into view. You are on center stage, surrounded by many sources. Avail yourself of them.

The guardian of a great soul!

■ Basic meaning

The essence of this card is in the consideration of spiritual needs. Note: the figure must become active in order to achieve this, namely turn round to see what's behind. Behind one's back is the domain of the subconscious. The figure must get to know—and then accept—each of his cups. This will release feelings, longings, beliefs, and from that moment on the card stands for his/your having taken account of spiritual needs and codes of values.

■ Spiritual experience

"Everything about you is valuable if you just take it into your possession." (Sheldon B. Kopp)

■ As the card for the day

Take a good look at what is going on inside you. You don't have to put it all on show!

■ As a prognosis/tendency

Satisfaction, enjoyment, peace, and harmony come from within you as a result of your saying "Yes" to yourself.

■ For love and relationships

This is not just about *your* feelings! Sometimes we just sit there, stuck fast; sometimes we worry endlessly. Let it flow! Stay true to love. Do something enjoyable together!

■ For success and happiness

You're a lucky child: you have confidence in yourself.

The 10 most important symbols

The figure's position or pose

At first sight: you with your partner, children, and your own house in the country. **And then:** your masculine and feminine sides. You as a child and as an adult. Prospects which come true or to which you reach out in vain.

Red—yellow—blue – ❶

Positive: you remain true to your original aims, origins, and motives. **Negative:** you pursue rather simple ends. You don't really make use of the broader possibilities in your life.

The pair / man and woman – ❷

Married life, partnership, including the partnership between one's masculine and feminine aspects. On the one hand an image of wholeness. On the other hand, we don't see the faces.

The two pairs – ❸

Positive: fruitful interaction between children and adults. Being able, as an adult, to be a child again. **Negative:** the adults pay no attention to the children. Appearances mean more than reality.

The rainbow

A sign of the beauty of creation, everyday miracles and one's personal creativity. **Task:** to allow heaven and earth, wishes, and reality to engage in a productive relationship with each other.

The Cups in the rainbow

Positive: the raised cups (cf. *The somewhat raised Cups,* p. 127). **Negative:** blown-up emotions. Nothing you can get hold of. A glass cover that makes a hermetic seal.

The house – ❹

A sign of home and a symbol for identity. The house is some distance away, half hidden. **Positive:** a large property, fulfillment of a wide range of needs. **Negative:** unclear situation, hidden identity, lack of profile.

Countryside – ❺

A symbol for both outer and inner nature and culture. This is about all spiritual needs and feelings. **Positive:** cultivated needs and passions. **Negative:** lack of culture, false modesty.

Back view

Negative: you have an ambivalent relationship with yourself. **Positive:** but you possess huge spiritual powers, needs, and passions that you don't need to be ashamed of.

The river – ❻

The river is part of the landscape. It is a matter of cultivating passions and emotions, and all other possible interpretations of the river apply here too: see the *Five of Cups, Eight of Cups, III - The Empress, IV - The Emperor* etc.

Ten of Cups

Man and woman, parents and children, man and his creation: The rainbow is symbolic of connectedness with God, with creation, of the fulfillment of great wishes—a sign of creativity and cultural fantasy. Everything contained in the image—each person, the landscape—also shows parts of yourself.

I'm in heaven…

■ **Basic meaning**

Highest beliefs, a mighty energy field—for good or ill. The faces are not visible. The cups are floating a long way away and form a kind of shield over everything. As a warning: the threat of losing oneself; intoxication or sterility; romanticism to be seen in the gestures; a symbolical let's pretend. Solution: acceptance of all available spiritual energies (Cups) so as to be able to work on them. Raise up your wishes and fears! Nature and culture are shown in the image as symbols of one's spiritual landscape, i.e., for cultivated passions. The card for the fulfillment of lifelong dreams.

■ **Spiritual experience**

High days and holidays, wedding, love-knot.

■ **As the card for the day**

Are you afraid of powerful emotions and high-flying dreams? Care-ful? With an exaggerated need for harmony?

■ **As a prognosis / tendency**

It will help to get your desires and fears sorted out. There are four steps to take …

■ **For love and relationships**

…fulfill worthwhile wishes, throw useless ones overboard, and

■ **For success and happiness**

…also take justified fears seriously and take appropriate measures as well as recognizing unjustified fears—which can then be sent packing.

The Swords

The 10 most important symbols

The figure's position or pose

A 'high-profile' personality, a mistress of sword-craft, of the weapons of the intellect. **The mirror tells us:** so, too, are we, and so shall we become.

The crown

A hard crown of gold adorns her head—and at the same time a wreath of butterflies. **Effortlessness, but at the same time resolution which can be relentless**—both aspects typical of the aerial element of the mind.

The butterflies – ❶

Lightness, but also flightiness. **Also:** a metaphor for the soul (the breath of life, psyche). A symbol for the successful metamorphosis from the caterpillar to the butterfly: **from a run-of-the-mill person to awareness and vitality.**

Child's head / sylph / elf – ❷

The inner child, childhood dreams, growing up in order to be able to fulfill these and to come to terms with the fears of childhood —however, all of this in the gray rock of the throne: perhaps an indication of repression and disregard.

The double ax – ❸

Two sickle moons (cf. the same symbol on the throne of the *King of Swords*). A sign of the matriarchy, ancient dynasties in which the female line held sway.

The bracelets – ❹

Decorative signs. Signs of emancipation or vanity. **But also:** sundered shackles.

Gray throne – ❺

The color gray signifies lack of prejudice, but also of awareness. Is the queen truly aware of her throne? She has the wind at her back, waters flow behind her—but does she know what moves her?

The curtain of clouds – ❻

Positive: freedom, weightlessness, on cloud nine, lightness, a bird's-eye view. **Negative:** head in the clouds, remoteness, nebulous goals.

Head above the clouds

Positive: knowledge, space, a citizen of two worlds (one's head in the heavens, feet on the earth). **Negative:** a warning against being too aloof, losing touch with reality.

A bird

In contrast to the other court cards of the Swords, which all depict several birds: **high-flying thoughts, love, wisdom, the ability to focus things, to find the common denominator.**

QUEEN OF SWORDS

You are like this queen. The card emphasizes your royal dignity and also your feminine attributes! You are developing a majestic mastery over the aerial forces. All your skills as a human being with new ideas, a good imagination and a love of fairness are needed.

Above the clouds…

■ Basic meaning

The mistress of the basic values, and clear—though loving—limits: "What is important in life? What do I want to live for?" As is the case with all the court cards, this queen represents an ideal, the perfect mastery over the element in question, in this case the Swords (air, words, thoughts, opinions). You are like this queen—or you are well on your way! And / or you are destined to meet somebody who personifies this *queen*.

■ Spiritual experience

The advantage and the difficulty of having the option, test of conscience, choosing the good, bursting the chains.

■ As the card for the day

Be clear in your decisions and your behavior. Make sure your point of view is thought through, and then stand by it with a sharp wit and self-possession.

■ As a prognosis / tendency

A card for reducing fears and for new openings in love.

■ For love and relationships

Try to understand what your heart wants! Garnish your love, lust, and passion with finesse and goodness of heart.

■ For success and happiness

Without exaggerated zeal, without anger and without trying to get others to acknowledge you … relax, and let your talent for careful work unfold itself!

The 10 most important symbols

The figure's position or pose

This king, master of the swords, sits immediately opposite us. He is our pattern and our ideal in matters of sovereignty and mastery.

The double sickle-moons – ❹

The night, feelings and dreams in their ever-changing forms. They form the backdrop, the motives and aims that need to be clarified with the help of the sword.

The light blue robe

He is an expression of the heavenly, spiritual dimension. And of yearning, the blues, the innermost part of the flame, which burns blue.

Head above the clouds

Positive: knowledge, space, a citizen of two worlds (one's head in the heavens, feet on the earth). **Negative:** a warning against being too aloof, losing touch with reality.

The inclined Sword – ❶

Is his sword nothing more than an extension of his moodiness and longings? Or is it the epitome of knowledge, and wisdom which gives us our happy facility in managing those longings and needs?

The gray mantle – ❺

The king's clothing is mainly light blue and red. **But:** the gray mantle can make all this disappear. Grayness can blanket *joie-de-vivre* and vivacity, but it may also be a sign of shrewdness and fairness.

The butterflies – ❷

Lightness, but also flightiness. **Also:** a metaphor for the soul (the breath of life, psyche). A symbol for the successful metamorphosis from the caterpillar to the butterfly: **from a run-of-the-mill person to awareness and vitality.**

The gray throne pointing skyward

The weapons of the intellect enable us to live a life of awareness. This is demonstrated by the throne, which builds a bridge between heaven and earth, desire and reality, theory and practice.

The couple—of people or elves – ❸

Love, happiness, and dance are the ingredients of the background. Albeit at the king's back; perhaps in his subconscious.

Two birds – ❻

High-flying ideas, a bird's-eye view, great plans. The number two: Coming to terms with oneself and with others.

KING OF SWORDS

You are like this king. The card emphasizes your royal dignity and also your masculine attributes! You have, and are, developing a majestic mastery over the aerial forces of life. Your whole potential as a human being with a sense of independence, clarity of thought, and farsightedness is needed.

Into the blue…

■ Basic meaning
The master of knowledge: "What do I know of life / of my partner / of this moment?" As is the case with all the court cards, this king represents an ideal, the perfect mastery over the element in question, in this case the Swords (air, words, thoughts, opinions). You are like this king—or you are well on your way! And/or you are destined to meet somebody who personifies this *king*.

■ Spiritual experience
The ability to grasp (complex) interconnections. Simplifying difficult matters.

■ As the card for the day
Make your contribution toward living life together harmoniously.

■ As a prognosis / tendency
This card describes strong mental forces, energies in the realms of the mind, knowledge, and conscience, which either emanate from you and / or which others try to bring to bear on you.

■ For love and relationships
What you really need is not to be achieved by calculated manipulation, nor by hiding behind intelligent lack of commitment. Stick to what genuinely affects you.

■ For success and happiness
Success or failure depends on our ability to question our own motives and see ourselves as others do, and how much we are able to understand other people's view of themselves and of us.

The 10 most important symbols

The figure's position or pose

 A high-profile personality riding to the left (from the observer's point of view) with his sword held high—i.e., into the realm of the subconscious.

The armor – ❶

 He is well equipped for conflict: either he is battling against the subconscious, which will turn him into a fanatic, **or he is a radical:** literally, one who is in search of his roots and in a hurry to find them.

Horse and rider

 The **gray horse** warns against indifference to instincts, the body, and its impulses. **Or:** it helps us adopt an attitude of conscious neutrality when it comes to rational discussion of instincts and drives.

The butterflies – ❷

 Lightness, but also flightiness. **Also:** a metaphor for the soul (the breath of life, psyche). A symbol for the successful metamorphosis from the caterpillar to the butterfly: from a run-of-the-mill person to awareness and vitality.

The red birds – ❸

 Positive: passionate thoughts, high-flying aims. **Negative:** warning against false zeal and a love (red) that blinds one or makes one see red.

Against the wind – ❹

 This knight is charging against the wind: He defies the (old) powers, creates his own fresh air. **Positive:** mental agility, enthusiasm takes wings. **Negative:** fanaticism, radicalism.

The Sword is greater than the image – ❺

 The great sword goes beyond the limits of the image. **Positive:** we grasp things way beyond our own horizons. **Negative:** we don't know what we have set loose ('the Sorcerer's Apprentice').

Red feathers / red cloth

 Dark red, deep emotions, high passion! **Positive:** a great love that overcomes a great deal! **Negative:** a warning against getting carried away by unconscious emotions.

A wide open field (earth, plowland) – ❻

 Shown almost bare of vegetation: **a warning** against becoming alienated from the earth. **Task:** to honor and pay tribute to creation using the sword, the weapon of the intellect (see the *Ace of Swords*).

Five birds

 Positive: the multifaceted and quintessential mind. **Negative:** lack of unity, lack of coherence.

KNIGHT OF SWORDS

You are like this knight. The card emphasizes your sovereignty and also your masculine attributes! You have and are developing a masterful, all-encompassing way of dealing with the aerial forces of life. Your whole determination as a human being with a good deal of curiosity and a sharp intellect is needed.

Quicker than the shadow...

■ Basic meaning

The master of insight: "What's behind it all? What's new? What happens in the end?" As is the case with all the court cards, this knight represents an ideal, the perfect mastery over the element in question, in this case the swords (air, words, thoughts, opinions). You are like this knight—or you are well on your way! And/or you are destined to meet somebody who personifies this *knight*.

■ Spiritual experience

The radicalness of those who truly love.

■ As the card for the day

Aims that turn you on, enabling you to focus your powers. That way you experience a lot and find success.

■ As a prognosis / tendency

You don't hide behind conventional dos and don'ts in order to get out of doing things. You realize your potential.

■ For love and relationships

What's needed now is your conscious affirmation of more love, humor, and joy. Simply more time, more ideas, more vision for your heart's desires!

■ For success and happiness

Could your value judgments use a clear-out? How about letting your thoughts roam outside of the box? Dare to commit yourself (more) and be more persistent.

The 10 most important symbols

The figure's position or pose

 Even the page fully commands the sword, the weapon of the mind. One leg is firmly placed on the ground, the other merely incidental. He looks into the wind and turns with it, either holding the sword back or about to strike.

Sky / clouds

 The sky is clearing and the wind is driving the clouds away. So the figure is also representative of a breath of fresh air and intellectual clarification.

A leg to stand on / the free leg – ❶

 Positive: alternation between play and industriousness, taking it lightly, and perseverance. **Negative:** indecisiveness, dillydallying, and flirtatiousness.

The Sword is greater than the image – ❷

 The great sword goes beyond the limits of the image. **Positive:** we grasp things way beyond our own horizons. **Negative:** we don't know what we have set loose ('the Sorcerer's Apprentice').

Red boots – ❸

 Negative: hotspur, fanaticism. **Positive:** willpower, enterprise, the opposite of a bloodless ghost.

Violet clothing – ❹

 Violet marks one of the limits of visible light (next to ultraviolet radiation, the unseen). **Positive:** frontier spirit. **Negative:** lack of respect, infringement of limits.

Yellow-green landscape – ❺

 Green: growth, nature, naturalness, freshness, hope, gradual development. **Yellow:** search for meaning, but also envy. Gold, but also greed.

Blue mountains

 A 'spiritual landscape': All parts of the scene are necessary—hills, valleys, near and far. Thus does that which is indicated by the blue mountains succeed: the marriage between heaven and earth, aspiration and reality.

Flock of birds – ❻

 Positive: brainstorming, creative and multifaceted thinking. **Negative:** idolization, absentmindedness, getting sidetracked, lack of focus.

The light blue sky

 The heavens = the divine realm and the realm of the will. **Light blue =** (open) sky; (clear) water. **Positive:** lightheartedness, spiritual joy, purpose of will, lucid mind. **Negative:** being over admiring, wishful thinking.

PAGE OF SWORDS

You are like this page. The card emphasizes your sovereignty and also your young and dynamic side! You have and are developing a masterful, innovative way of dealing with the aerial forces of life. All your skills as a human being with a spirit and a discriminating mind are needed.

Hold on to what brings you clarity!

■ Basic meaning

The adventure of ideas and insights: "What's happening? How is it going? What do I think about that?" As is the case with all the court cards, this page represents an ideal, the perfect mastery over the element in question, in this case the swords (air, words, thoughts, opinions). You are like this page—or you are well on your way! And/or you are destined to meet somebody who personifies this *page*.

■ Spiritual experience

Surprise yourself. Stay alert. Think beyond your own limitations.

■ As the card for the day

Get an overview of what's going on, show initiative, and present your thoughts and ideas to the world.

■ As a prognosis/tendency

This card points the way to innovation and unconventional, experimental thinking. And it warns against gullibility and ignorance. You gain mastery over the sword!

■ For love and relationships

Love in every way...Have the courage to trust yourself—there are more ways and possibilities than you think!

■ For success and happiness

Love is an attitude. Try it at work and in the home—you will achieve much more that way than any other!

The 10 most important symbols

The card as a mirror

We are like the Sword. A sharp intellect is double-edged. Mankind and his level of consciousness may represent the crown of creation, but not yet the peak of progress.

The blue-white Sword

Feeling and inflexibility, spirituality and intellect are the governing aspects of the sword. **Task:** to recognize and master its double character. To prevent injury and to heal, to make light of difficulties.

The hand emerging from the cloud – ❶

The sword is a gift to you. You are yourself a gift—for yourself and for the world. Accept it and make something of it. Grasp it, handle it and let your intellect shine.

The six drops of gold – ❷

The divine spark, the spark of consciousness—in a religious sense the Holy Ghost. The number 6 is also a reference to the card *VI - The Lovers:* the story of Paradise lost and Paradise regained!

The gray sky

Positive: neutral, objective, composed, without prejudice, balanced, fair. **Negative:** clouded thinking, unconscious, apathetic, expressionless.

The golden crown – ❸

We see a four-point crown: the tip of the sword makes five, which symbolizes the quintessence—the fifth power—a spirit which heals is the quintessence of experiences that we have been through!

The twigs – ❹

Negative: alienation and destruction. The sword plunders nature. **Positive:** elevation, coronation and celebration of nature through the gift of consciousness. Respect for and appreciation of our natural resources.

The blue-violet mountains – ❺

Here they are indicative of abstraction, of a mental overview. **Negative:** theory is more important than practical well-being. **Positive:** one is not a stick-in-the-mud, but is prepared to see the other side.

The peak – ❻

The border between heaven and earth. The symbolic home of mankind as citizens of two worlds. **Task:** clarify your aims in life, make a conscious decision as to which peak you wish to reach.

The heights / atmosphere

"There are more things in heaven and earth, Horatio,/Than are dreamt of in your philosophy." (William Shakespeare). All the aces remind us that it is a good idea to get to know this in-between world—and we can do it!

ACE OF SWORDS

A gift of life: the Sword symbolizes mental independence, the acuteness of intellect, our words, our thoughts and opinions. The Swords symbolize human evolution in its full span between being the crown of creation—and its greatest hazard.

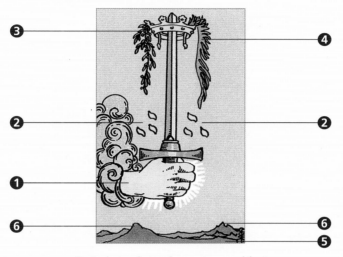

Praise be to what makes us strong and free!

■ Basic meaning

The Swords are the weapons of the intellect, words, thoughts, and opinions: here we have to do with mental activity, with recognition, understanding, and learning—basically with everything that makes life easier to live. The essential thing is that things are *clear* or *become* clear. The key term is "spirit," for in contrast to mere intellect, the spirit is able to find its way right down to the essence of a person or an issue. The Ace provides an elementary way in—it's all yours!

■ Spiritual experience

Healing old wounds through love and awareness.

■ As the card for the day

Rise up, stand up straight, and benefit from a new clarity!

■ As a prognosis / tendency

You find an opportunity to clarify hitherto undefined desires and fears and to improve your quality of life.

■ For love and relationships

"Love looks not with the eyes but with the mind." (William Shakespeare)
A great-minded life is one lived in and with conscious love.

■ For success and happiness

You have and you need a good capacity for thought and staying power. Brain jogging and physical exercise are good ways of supporting your knightliness.

The 10 most important symbols

The figure's position or pose

Upright, the legs slightly apart, the arms folded in front of the chest. There is a good flow within the body from top to bottom and vice versa. **Or:** the person has a blockage from the breast upwards.

The blindfold – ❶

The realm of the mind extends far beyond the physically visible. Indeed, it really only begins where physical vision stops. **Negative:** under a delusion, not knowing what is going on. **Positive:** mental activity, lack of prejudice.

The reach of the Swords – ❷

Think global—act local! The unconditionality and the freedom of the mind should remain in contact with the conditionality, i.e., with the practical necessities of existence. **Also:** a broad mental horizon.

The crossed arms – ❸

The breast contains the heart and—according to widespread opinion—the soul. **Positive:** all thoughts radiate from here and come back here to roost. **Negative:** blockage, limitation.

The white patch on the forehead – ❹

A reference to the third eye, the higher insights that we achieve when we are able to endure the balance between land and water—dream and reality.

The gray of the figure

Positive: neutral, objective, composed, without prejudice, balanced, fair. **Negative:** clouded thinking, unconscious, apathetic, expressionless.

The wide waters

Endless waters, the hydrologic cycle, surging feelings. They are all there—the question is simply whether the figure in the image has noticed them at his or her back, i.e., whether he or she consciously takes them into account.

The sickle moon

It is wise to turn around and be conscious of what is behind one, otherwise the moon with its intuitions, but also its moods, can cause confusion. **Also:** "…interpret, and then live one's dreams!"

The islands or rocks – ❺

The isles of consciousness in the ocean of the subconscious (an image suggested by Sigmund Freud). **Also:** the ability to draw conclusions about that which is hidden below the surface on the basis of what is visible.

The other shore – ❻

The task or ability to see the other side, i.e. to perceive the unknown and the unconscious in oneself and in others, and to be tolerant of differentness.

Two of Swords

The Swords—the weapons of the intellect—are spread wide and extend beyond the given frame. Moon and water stand for feelings, spirituality, and generally for the sheer breadth of life. However, this part of the soul lies at the figure's back, perhaps unknown, below the level of consciousness.

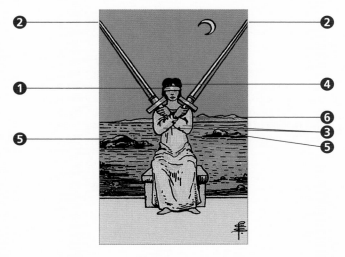

One can see clearly only with the heart. (A. de Saint-Exupéry)

■ Basic meaning

The blindfold over the eyes represents a warning against failing to grasp an issue and against holding prejudices. In a positive sense, it stands for impartiality and preparation for *seeing things with the mind's eye*. For the realm of the mind and spirit starts where the physical eye can no longer discern, and that is where you deal with the most important issues.

■ Spiritual experience

Between the day and the dream…on a frontier between the soul and the intellect.

■ As the card for the day

Don't put up a smoke screen. Dare to explore and look inside yourself, go beyond the obvious.

■ As a prognosis / tendency

It's not worth playing blind man's buff. Reality doesn't just consist of one-way streets or throwaway solutions.

■ For love and relationships

Blow the dust off your fantasy and try using your imagination more. That way you can get rid of the 'gray areas' of your relationship.

■ For success and happiness

Take care of this borderline region between the conscious and the subconscious—and you will never run out of new ideas and creative solutions!

The 10 most important symbols

No figure is depicted.

 And yet one part of the human body is seen in close-up. What is shown in *III - The Empress* is repeated here on the level of the swords: thrusting through to the essentials, bringing together heart and mind.

The card as a mirror I

 The shading in the image could represent rain. One feels wounded, suffering, the atmosphere is dismal. "It's raining in my heart," says the song.

The card as a mirror II

 Equally, though, the shading indicates a mirror. The clouds of fog recede. Just as when Eros' arrow pierces our heart, we feel smitten, but light and full of enthusiasm!

The proportions

 In comparison with the rest, the heart is shown large, while the swords are rather small. You have a big heart! Be proud of it! Defend yourself and don't let mere pinpricks have an influence on you!

The heart – ❶

 Our whole heritage, and all our possibilities are in our blood. They are our birthright—inheritance and also assignment. Just as with all other feelings, the emotions of the heart are not automatically positive.

The Swords – ❷

 The purpose of the swords is therefore precisely to help us sort out our affairs of the heart, make the right choices and to put a name to things—in short, find the right perspective.

The composition

 Together, the swords and the heart form the interface which joins the heart with the intellect. From a psychological point of view, this represents the basis of consciousness. **In practice, this means:** getting to the point!

The clouds – ❸

 Rain, fog, uncertainty. **But also:** that state of consciousness—the union of heart and mind—which allows us to do away with pointless pipe dreams and realize truly worthwhile, satisfying visions.

The shading – ❹

 On the one hand rain, on the hand representative of a mirror. Whereby rain is not only a sign of sadness and sorrows. From ancient times it has also been seen as a bond between heaven and earth.

The gray sky

 Positive: neutral, objective, composed, without prejudice, balanced, fair. **Negative:** clouded thinking, unconscious, apathetic, expressionless.

THREE OF SWORDS

The three swords stab through the heart. What can this mean other than pain, harm, sorrow? But we also know the image of Eros and the arrows that he shoots into our heart. Generally we have a positive attitude to the god of love and his habits—apparently being love-struck does us good!

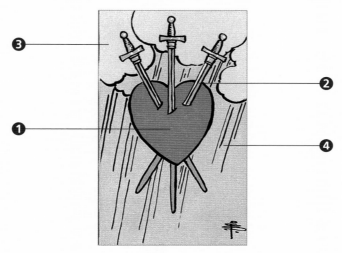

The interface—the heart meets up with the weapons of the intellect.

■ Basic meaning

The spheres of the mind / intellect (Swords) and the heart meet up and combine inextricably. Conscious thought finds its way into the recesses of the heart's domain. Thus what was only germinal, elusively intuited by the heart, is made clear and brought onto the conscious plane by the Swords. You comprehend what your heart is trying to tell you and what you need to do about it!

■ Spiritual experience

Understanding what keeps the world together on the deepest levels.

■ As the card for the day

Shine a light onto your recollections and expectations. Participation brings reward.

■ As a prognosis / tendency

"Don't let your heart become a murderer's pit." Wounds heal when they are treated properly.

■ For love and relationships

Give love a chance—including your love of truth and honesty.

■ For success and happiness

Caring instead of careworn!

The 10 most important symbols

The figure's position or pose

Paralysis, petrification, lifelessness, rigidity, exhaustion, deep sleep, prayer, memorial. **But on the other hand:** a mental journey, peace, deep meditation, intense concentration, inspiring mental energy, high tension.

The prone figure I – ❶

Sarcophagus, saint worship, martyrdom, hero's death, human harshness, wrong thoughts. Intensive care, anesthetic, fakir, Snow White after she bit into the poisoned apple. Shock, trauma. Under pressure.

The prone figure II

Psychiatrist's couch, a monk's bed, a cure, the spiritual life, mental alertness, descending into deeper layers of consciousness. The body at rest while the mind works overtime.

The prone figure III

Sleep, living in a dream world—the dream can be seen in the stained glass window. Danger of self-deception. **Positive:** imag(e)–ination—many experiences form the full picture. Conscious sleep and dreaming.

The color gray

Positive: neutral, objective, composed, without prejudice, balanced, fair. **Negative:** clouded thinking, delusion, hermetically sealed. Unconscious, apathetic, expressionless.

The color yellow

Here a *dirty* yellow—yellow with some black mixed in. **Sun with shadow:** a state of consciousness that has a connection with the depths. It could also signify fever, mental problems, lack of clarity.

The arrangement of the Swords – ❷

Positive: well-sorted-out thoughts and insights. Experiences get worked through. Concentrated, unbiased, abstract thinking. **Negative:** ungrasped thoughts, unused weapons of the mind.

The mosaic / puzzle – ❸

Positive: working through experiences and getting them into perspective. Solving puzzles (in life). Recognizing patterns. Detailed knowledge. **Negative:** fragmented memories, suppositions, figments of the imagination.

The window – ❹

The contrasts (and overcoming them) between inner and outer issues, the abstract world and daily life, perfect ideals and limited reality. **Positive:** insight and understanding. **Negative:** the world remains outside.

The word 'PAX' – ❺

Latin for peace. **Positive:** contentment, mental tranquility, mental achievement. Deep satisfaction. Happiness. Peace of mind. **Negative:** fear of conflict, withdrawal, escaping into a world of fantasy.

FOUR OF SWORDS

An image of immense mental concentration and of a clear, calm conscience.
Or of rigidity, paralyzing thoughts, numbness. The human mind functions
in the same way as respiration: It is calm and relaxed when it is allowed to
proceed undisturbed in its own rhythm.

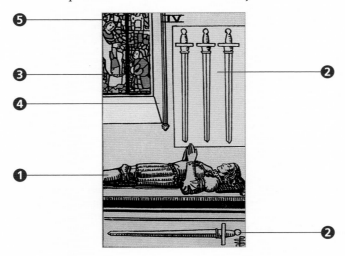

Fossilized … stoned … deep sleep … meditation …

■ Basic meaning

There is a danger of 'real life' and mental endeavor parting company: something is frozen—the energy of physical and / or mental activity. Seen positively, the mind finds access to deeper levels of contemplation, at last it finds peace and quiet for work. This is where experiences can be digested and thoughts pursued to their conclusions, fragments put together to form a coherent whole (stained glass window) and puzzles solved. The word PAX—peace—is visible in the window.

■ Spiritual experience

Satisfaction, deep relaxation, lucid dream, mental/spiritual journey.

■ As the card for the day

Allow yourself some peace and quiet! Use your mental potential, activate unused mental resources. You have quite a range of irons in the fire!

■ As a prognosis / tendency

You can master even major contradictions and clarify challenging incongruities. Relax, so that your mind can focus on the issue.

■ For love and relationships

Give yourself a chance to calm down by letting go of envy, jealousy, and over-enthusiasm.

■ For success and happiness

Let your mind work in all directions. What is occupying your attention contains some big ideas!

The 10 most important symbols

The figures' position or poses

 Large, medium, tiny—this could mark the stations of a very personal development. Equally, a scene showing a certain encounter or confrontation with others.

The backward glance – ❶

 The large figure looks back at the other two: **Negative:** arrogance, meanness, wishing others ill. **Positive:** regard, participation, consideration, satisfaction over one's growth.

The three figures I – ❷

 A development in three stages, from small to large: A difficult start—the problems seemed to flood in, one felt very small without the support of the swords—head in one's hands…

The three figures II – ❸

 …and then a more mature stage, another perspective. The figure in the foreground can look after himself (with *Three Swords*); looking back, he understands more clearly how past problems arose and how to avoid them in future.

The three figures III – ❹

 The story of the three figures can also be told the other way around: from large to small, back to the roots, to the source, return, recall, the search for the wellspring of life.

At the water's edge

 The link between intellect and feelings (air and water). **Negative:** bad feelings get fought out with the help of swords. **Positive:** problems are solved and needs fulfilled using the weapons of the intellect.

The clouds

 Positive: the gray clouds are dispersing, the sky is clearing. A fresh breeze, sweet air. **Negative:** the blue sky is disappearing behind clouds—false or foggy mental aims, and discord is in the air.

Three plus two Swords – ❺

 Negative: uncompleted mental efforts—some of the weapons of the intellect remain unused—half-truths. **Positive:** doubts can be overcome (two swords), one works on the information which one has (three swords).

The colors red and green

 Lifeblood and nature/growth/ripeness. **Negative:** over-keenness, envy, taking malicious pleasure in others' bad luck, immaturity. **Positive:** will and potential for growth, learning and joy in progress and development.

The islands/shore – ❻

 Negative: uneven and irregular knowledge, islands of awareness in a sea of ignorance. **Positive:** an opposite shore, taking account of a contrary stance, seeing the other side/point of view, overcoming difficulties.

FIVE OF SWORDS

The large figure in the picture prevails over the two smaller ones—this may be just and good, or the result of injustice and ruthlessness. Or the image shows three stages of development. Looking back, it is possible to understand the causes of earlier difficulties and avoid repeating them.

The quintessence of the Swords—learning from experience!

■ Basic meaning

Seen in a positive light, the image portrays a process of growth and healing: at first you were practically swimming and the support that the swords could supply was unknown to you (at your back); holding your head in your hands seemed to be the only thing to do. Then you grew in knowledge and experience. Today you are larger than ever: now you have all the swords at your disposal and are content in your store of knowledge. Looking back, you know that you can do away with yesterday's doubts and weaknesses.

■ Spiritual experience

Giving up habits and the subconscious urge to relive past emotions.

■ As the card for the day

Look at both triumph and disaster and try to see their deeper significance. Make use of the weapons of the intellect as a means of healing.

■ As a prognosis / tendency

It is never too late—and seldom too early—to work through emotions and to learn from them. You will learn a lot.

■ For love and relationships

Don't let difficulties get you down. Stand up for clarity and uprightness.

■ For success and happiness

Let your knowledge bear fruit. Note the two swords on the ground: beware of (making) empty promises and of unfounded assumptions.

The 10 most important symbols

The figure's position or poses

Three people are all in the same boat, and they personify effort, devotion, and *laissez-faire*. The boat is (also) a common metaphor for the control exercised by the conscious mind on the waters of the subconscious.

The ferryman

Positive: the mediator between the worlds (like Hermann Hesse's ferryman in *Siddharta*). **Negative:** lack of redemption, restlessness, homelessness (like the ferryman in the Brothers Grimm's *The Devil with the Three Golden Hairs*).

The figure I – ❶

Your masculine side, the active part, the conscious act. **Danger:** being a know-it-all, making decisions for others. Control fixation. **Positive:** shouldering responsibility, not being fatalistic, prepared to give of one's all.

The figure II – ❷

Your feminine side, the passive part, conscious dedication. **Danger:** indecision, feeling inferior, letting others decide. **Positive:** being open for how things develop, patience.

The figure III – ❸

Your child side, the unconscious decision; what happens to you. **Danger:** being dependent, not self-reliant, unpleasant surprises. **Positive:** curiosity, open for new experiences, wonder.

The black pole – ❹

Progress through keeping on the ground (back to the basics). **Positive:** getting to the bottom of things, thoroughness. **Negative:** black = the unknown: the motives and reasons remain part of your blind spot.

The six Swords – ❺

Negative: old prejudices are dragged on into every new situation—mental ballast obscures the view. **Positive:** the weapons of the intellect as compass needles, conscious experience, consistency in change.

The back view

Negative: turning one's back on oneself, a mental one-way-street. **Positive:** the conscious perception of the other side of the coin from the observer's point of view, investigation of unconscious motives.

Two different waters – ❻

Moving and still waters: old and new, the task of consciously bringing about change and the transition of form.

The colors blue and gray

Positive: neutrality, lack of bias, lack of prejudice, serenity, clear will and mind. **Negative:** lack of awareness, apathy, muddied thought, sticking to old judgments, repetition, need for some fresh air.

Six of Swords

At first sight we see a journey from A to B. It also shows the strength and the mission of the intellect to form a link between worlds, to remain alert and to keep up with what is going on. Literally, the word translation means carrying across, i.e. 'transporting' sense from one language to another.

The lot of the ferryman.

■ Basic meaning

Connecting worlds, having understanding for what is foreign (including understanding men, women, children as individuals). The black pole is a decisive symbol: the boat only moves when the pole touches the very bottom. In the language of tarot: success comes from keeping in touch with the basics. (Otherwise the cargo of swords is just old ballast being moved from one place to the next.) Knowing one's basic motives and aims enriches contacts with others and is a great navigation aid (the swords in the bow).

■ Spiritual experience

Fundamental experiences such as love, death, plenty or lack.

■ As the card for the day

Try to get to the bottom of differences of opinion. Make sure you 'get across' what is important to you.

■ As a prognosis / tendency

"When you know what you're doing you can do what you like." (Moshé Feldenkrais) The promise of the image is a lively consciousness and …

■ For love and relationships

… knowing when you are going with the flow, sensing flow within you and between yourself and others and …

■ For success and happiness

… learning how to chart your own course in the river of time and events.

The 10 most important symbols

The figure's position or pose

The figure's strange posture is both riddle and answer at once: running ahead and glancing back. With careful movements, which perhaps go round in circles.

Five and two Swords – ❶

You act according to / with that which you can grasp. **Negative:** you leave something important behind (two swords) that belong to you. **Positive:** you leave doubts (the two swords) behind you.

The figure's posture I – ❷

Running ahead and glancing back: a sign of inner conflict, the unconscious, unreliability: while signaling left you turn right. A contradiction in person, a living conundrum.

The figure's posture II

An image of conscious living, as expressed in the citation from Kierkegaard overleaf. It is about consciously deciding on one's own path in life (the Major Card *VII - The Chariot* shown here on the Swords level).

On tip-toe – ❸

The essential thing is to develop a way of doing things with care—at a walking pace. The figure's gait—walking on the balls of his feet—indicates this awareness. Also, the image is a warning against stealth and surprises that come soft of foot.

The tents – ❹

Negative: unrest, homelessness, a nomadic life, always under way and never at home. **Positive:** life keeps moving, peace and continuity in the context of change, feeling at home wherever one may be.

The group of people – ❺

Negative: the main figure looks down (condescendingly?) on his fellows. **Positive:** being clear about one's own role / task. We spend a lot of time arguing with others because we lack the courage to live our dreams.

Red shoes / red hat – ❻

Red stands for the will, passion, lifeblood. **Negative:** willfulness from head to toe, moods that go to the head and the feet. **Positive:** an affair of the heart, a heart's desire that one pursues with both willpower and ardor.

Yellow

Bright sunlight, but also envy and the search for meaning. **Danger:** coming too close to the sun can provoke a fall (into mania or delusion). **Positive:** illumination of the opposite side as well = strong, reliable consciousness.

Sandy / earthen color

Down to earth, material, substance. Conscious awareness knows about its natural foundations; unconscious existence runs blind.

SEVEN OF SWORDS

The depicted figure is running ahead and looking backwards. Either his view —his behavior—is displaced, or the image expresses, on the contrary, an indisputable and important aphorism: "One has to live life forwards, but one can only understand it backwards." (Sören Kierkegaard)

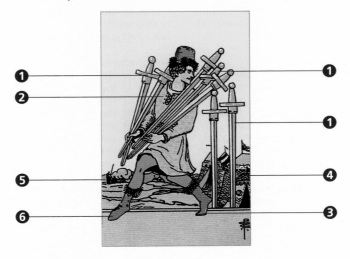

Uplifting contradictions.

■ Basic meaning

The card for conscious living, for spiritual self-experience, sometimes for losing oneself in the mysteries of one's own life. The tents stand for mobile living. They are a warning against being too nomadic in life (always under way and never at home). And they encourage one to be flexible (to feel at home wherever one happens to be), to accept change and progress.

■ Spiritual experience

Leaving self-doubt and old behavior patterns behind one… understanding the meaning of one's personal riddles… finding an important solution!

■ As the card for the day

"That's how we've done it for the past twenty years!" "Maybe, but you could have been doing it wrong for the past twenty years!"

■ As a prognosis / tendency

The figure takes five swords. The Swords' quintessence is: take time to learn, heal old wounds with new solutions. Two swords are left: doubts or 'leftovers'.

■ For love and relationships

Allow yourself—and others—to do an irrational, nonsensical, crazy thing.

■ For success and happiness

Have the courage of your dreams—and the strength to face the unsolved puzzles of your life.

The 10 most important symbols

The figure's position or pose

Bound up or duty bound? You are caught up by the weapons of the intellect. **Or:** beyond what seems to be and beyond what can be grasped begins the realm of personal consequence.

The blindfold – ❶

Negative: unable to see what is going on, gray area, only able to see one point of view. **Positive:** justice, lack of bias, impartiality, not being taken in by appearances. Connection between the two sides of the brain.

Bonds around the arms and legs – ❷

Negative: embarrassment (French: *embarrasser*, to block, to obstruct), immobility, can't grasp things, stiff, don't touch, don't bend down. **Positive:** steadfast, not grasping, giving up old habits, reinforcement of the center.

Bindings around head and hands – ❸

Link between thought and act, head and body or gut feeling. **Negative:** bondage. **Positive:** binding loyalty/obligingness—duty bound. **Also:** a time of withdrawal within oneself, letting the blinds down.

The mountain – ❹

Conscious letting go gives the inner will knowledge and space to unfold itself.—He who plumbs his own depths finds it easier then to rise up high. Difficulties—and overcoming them.

The castle – ❺

Negative: cutting oneself off, imprisonment, isolation. Shut off from the rest of the world. **Also:** mother fixation. **Positive:** protection, independence, safety, strong identity. Looking after oneself. Finding security within oneself.

Water and earth

Negative: withered feelings. **Also:** mud, sludge, morass of unconscious needs. **Positive:** all life emerges from water, earth and the sun. Conscious interaction with one's own basics and aims.

The encircling Swords – ❻

You *possess* the swords and the power to free yourself from undesirable bonds. **And:** the weapons of the intellect are your fortress, giving you security and protection in your life!

The clothing

Red for lifeblood and the will. Beige for the color of the body. The needs of body and will are curbed, controlled, held captive by the swords—or rather strengthened and given reliable support.

The gray sky

Positive: neutral, objective, composed, conscious (and highly focused). **Negative:** bad atmosphere, taking sides, quarrelsome. **Or:** unconscious, unwilling to participate, expressionless (and apathetic).

EIGHT OF SWORDS

EIGHT OF SWORDS

When you feel bound, caught up with things, it is a positive step to become aware of this. The Swords give you the means to cut through the bonds. On the other hand, the card is also a pointer to times for reflection, times to spin a cocoon and let something new develop and hatch out.

Cast off bonds and obligations.

■ Basic meaning

This card stands for *bindings*—the bonds of duty, the bond between thinking and doing: doing what one says, and indeed doing what one thinks. In that respect an expression of a certain consequence. "There are thoughts which you cannot grasp without changing your life." (Werner Sprenger) And: you won't be able to change some things in your life without having grasped your thoughts. Thinking is a process characterized by the way it transcends material things and what seems to exist.

■ Spiritual experience

The acceptance of personal limits—doing away with spiritual confines!

■ As the card for the day

In your present situation neither what seems to be, nor habitual behavior, nor an instinctive will are going to get you any further.

■ As a prognosis / tendency

Unsuitable convictions are fetters; appropriate ones can liberate and strengthen.

■ For love and relationships

A departure from head-in-the-clouds behavior and childish inhibitions.

■ For success and happiness

Have confidence in your own logic, do away with obligations that hinder you on your way, be consistent—with yourself and others!

The 10 most important symbols

The figure's position or pose

 A scene of sudden wakening or shock, darkness or illumination. There is a method for training the eyes (Throw away your glasses!) that starts in exactly the same way as shown in the picture, with so-called palming.

It's getting dark

 The black shadows stand for all that is unknown—whether because it has been suppressed and forgotten or because it is beyond one's ken, completely new territory, unforeseen tasks or experiences.

Light dawns

 It was dark. And in the darkness a light appears—in fact nine light projectors, mental flashes of inspiration, the swords as the weapons of the intellect. Take your time, but make sure you get used to the new insights.

The hands in front of the face I – ❶

 Get used to the new insights and knowledge. Take the time that's needed. Relax (in the palming process mentioned above things appear all the blacker the more we relax while doing it).

The hands in front of the face II

 If the pose is caused by a frightening experience, take your time as well. A whole mental horizon now appears in a new light. Don't close your eyes to it—that won't help here.

The pair of twins – ❷

 Negative: inner discord, belligerence, being self-opinionated, not being prepared to see the other side. **Positive:** coming to terms with inner conflict, being prepared to learn and change one's spots.

The quilt I – ❸

 The roses stand for the beauty and authenticity of the inner self—what really moves your heart and what would like to come to fruition within you. Here you can find your point of departure and of return.

The quilt I

 The collection of signs of the zodiac and planetary symbols do not have a special astrological significance. The point is that a whole cosmos, a complete cycle or integrated whole is to be considered here.

The Swords as bars – ❹

 We are not dealing with isolated thoughts—here there is a whole pattern involved. A complete mental horizon is obscured. A completely new network of insights comes into the foreground.

The contrasting colors black and white-blue

 In the Genesis story of the bible, God used one of the six days of creation to sort original chaos into black and white. It remains a great creative act for ourselves when we succeed in re-sorting black and white!

NINE OF SWORDS

The middle of the night—you are startled out of sleep, nightmares, undigested thoughts: get up and work out what you can do about it! It is dark, and many lights appear: mental flashes, nine Swords: a whole gamut of new knowledge and insights: get used to them carefully!

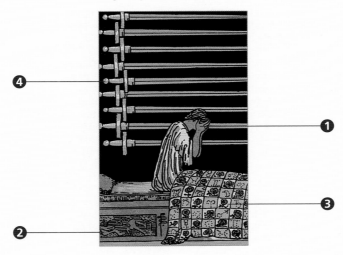

Shock or an illuminating awakening…

■ Basic meaning

Old horizons darken over—new ones lighten up. Fresh mental pastures. Seek and find words to describe impressions that up to now have left you speechless. Go further in your thoughts than you have so far. Become aware of events which still need to be processed. To distinguish between day and night, the definition of black and white is a huge creative act when as a result chaos is tamed, but a nightmare when it simply means that prejudice becomes cemented.

■ Spiritual experience

Awakening, experience of the divine, thinking beyond one's own horizons.

■ As the card for the day

Strengthen your sense of responsibility, your patience, and your trust. Don't let yourself be overmuch disheartened by temporary blockages or difficulties.

■ As a prognosis / tendency

"He who has grasped his situation cannot readily be restrained." (B. Brecht)

■ For love and relationships

Look at the roses in the image. Your soul is made to bloom and grow. There are so many people who are waiting to receive your love and who wish to give theirs to you.

■ For success and happiness

So put two and two together! Take a thorough look at the contradictions surrounding you.

The 10 most important symbols

The figure's position or pose

A warning against sacrifice and destruction. An encouragement for devotion and love. The totality of the swords—the mental talents—shows not a philosopher on his throne, but triumph over idols and models.

The red cloth I – ❶

The negative side of this card does not deal with death (which topic is dealt with in the card *XIII-Death*), but rather holding fast to previous judgments and illusions, even if they end in disaster.

The red cloth II

The red cloth stands for the flow of lifeblood in a person as well as from generation to generation. **Negative:** sticking obstinately to old theories. **Positive:** drawing new conclusions from old experiences!

A new horizon – ❷

Both from a positive and from a negative point of view, the methods employed so far get us no further. The fruits of knowledge consist in new decisions which open up new opportunities for love and awareness.

The sky I

The strong contrast between black and yellow is an indication of massive problems or tensions which are waiting to be or have just been addressed. A change of perspective—the thunderstorm is brewing—or just past.

The sky II

Sundown: the black (something suppressed or unknown) becomes apparent. **Sunrise:** A new sun, a new day. Each of these images can be seen in a positive or negative light.

The ten Swords – ❸

The seeds of the intellect are sprouting. False thoughts mean checkmate. Good, functioning thoughts bring light into the darkness. They bring us further along the path when all our ideals have failed.

'Nailed down' – ❹

The weapons of the intellect often nail us down. Only when our thoughts manifest themselves in flesh and blood do they escape from the realms of theory. There's nothing like putting things to a practical test…

The sign of blessing – ❺

(cf. the cards *V-The Hierophant, Six of Pentacles)* **Negative:** ill-used mental/spiritual powers can be very destructive—even a divine blessing. **Positive:** this is a specially potent card of blessing.

On the water's edge

Down by the riverside: at times of disaster or collapse we need the water of life. Spiritual powers and spirituality are like the fountain of youth when we give them a chance to flow!

TEN OF SWORDS

Look at the high-number Sword cards as a process of transformation from the caterpillar to the butterfly: in the Eight of Swords the caterpillar spins its cocoon. The Nine of Swords shows the process of attaining maturity in seclusion; and the Ten of Swords symbolizes the successful launch into a new dimension.

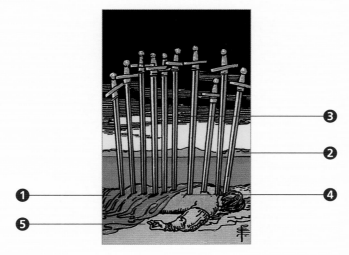

Out for the count…

■ Basic meaning

A scene in which the seed of the mind comes to fruition—for good or for evil. In a negative sense the swords as the weapons of the intellect are *always* representative of the destructive mind, of alienation from nature. This injurious aspect of the swords culminates here in this card. The positive side: as the peak of cognition the card does not portray a wise man, guru or philosophical ruler on his throne. On the contrary, the image heralds *the end of all idols and idolatry.*

■ Spiritual experience

"It is as it is, says Love." (Erich Fried)

■ As the card for the day

The road goes on beyond the horizon. Call a halt to the old ways. New possibilities, new paths are waiting!

■ As a prognosis / tendency

"If you meet the Buddha on your way, kill him." (Linji) The mental victory over idols and examples: nothing from the past can fully prepare you for what is to come.

■ For love and relationships

Something new is afoot in love and relationships, too. Be careful about drawing conclusions too quickly.

■ For success and happiness

You will achieve most with "peace of mind and presence of mind" (Ingrid Riedel). Take a couple of deep breaths!

The Pentacles / Coins

The 10 most important symbols

The figure's position or pose

Stooping and/or leaning (having a leaning toward something). Nonetheless upright, majestic. Attentive or concerned look. Her head is on one side/ the look directed. There is much at her back: in reserve or forgotten.

The Pentacle in the lap – ❶

Positive: you take care of talents, practical needs and tasks. **Negative:** you fail to grow because you lose track and concentrate too much on superficialities and what seems obvious.

Blossoms/Fruits – ❷

A sign of a good way of dealing with values, talents, and materials. The wealth of blossoms and fruits in the image show the queen's productivity, naturalness, and creativity. This applies both to the inner and outer nature.

The rose garden – ❸

Only here and in *I-The Magician:* the rose garden. **Promise:** a sign of fruitfulness, an auspicious situation. **Warning** against false ambition and also against false modesty.

The rabbit – ❹

Fertility (breeds prolifically). Giving space to animals = allowing space for drives and instincts. Love of all that is alive. What is small, petty—positive or negative complement to the blossoms in the sky.

The goat/the ibex – ❺

Ability to survive even in arid, barren country. The ibex lives high up in the mountains, on the border between heaven and earth. **Warning:** acting the goat; that gets my goat.

The blue mountains – ❻

Positive: this queen is an expert when it comes to creating heaven on earth. **Negative:** like many other aspects, the blue mountains are at her back. To take heed of them she first has to turn around.

The valley

It is unclear what exactly is to be found down there. **Positive:** keeping one's distance, the overview, mastery over one's own values and talents. **Negative:** too great a distance, outsider, close-fistedness.

The gray throne

Gray stands for neutrality. **Positive:** conscious equanimity. **Negative:** lack of respect for what is gray on the throne: goat or ibex heads, farther up a child's head and fruits like apples and pears.

Red—white—green

The image is more colorful than many others. Like the rose garden, the red and white robe alludes to *the Magician.* The green mantle stands for naturalness, freshness, and growth, while also warning against immaturity.

QUEEN OF PENTACLES / COINS

You are like this queen. The card emphasizes your royal dignity and also your feminine attributes! You have and are developing a majestic mastery over the earth forces of life. All your skills as a human being with a wealth of talent, realism, and sense of caring are needed.

At the foot of the blue mountains there is a rose garden.

■ **Basic meaning**

The mistress of the basic needs: "What do I need? What am I going to live on?" As is the case with all the court cards, this queen represents an ideal, the perfect mastery over the element in question, in this case the pentacles (earth, material, money, talent, the physical). You are like this queen—or you are well on your way! And/or you are destined to meet somebody who personifies this *queen.*

■ **Spiritual experience**

Discovering the wonder that is life and the wealth of creation in everyday things!

■ **As the card for the day**

"First do what's necessary, then what's possible, and suddenly you're doing the impossible." (old saying)

■ **As a prognosis / tendency**

The Queen of Pentacles signifies a power within us that can carry us up to peak experiences and the highest levels of performance!

■ **For love and relationships**

Love and respect for the essentials transform boring daily routine into a rose garden!

■ **For success and happiness**

It may be necessary to make special efforts to reach a higher level. Although it may also be necessary first of all to climb down from your pedestal!

The 10 most important symbols

The figure's position or pose

The king's eyes are shut or he is looking down: sleepy or pleasantly sunk in thought. The pose displays openness, but also a person who has become one with his mission.

The grapes I – ❶

Grapes and wine = sublime enjoyment: the sensory pleasures and joys of sensuality (Dionysian, the wine god Bacchus or Dionysos) and taking pleasure in the pursuit of meaning and truth (Apollonian; 'in vino veritas').

The grapes II

For time immemorial grapes have also symbolized gruelingly hard work—the laborers in the vineyard provide a lasting image of what it means to earn one's living with the sweat of one's brow.

The castle – ❷

Positive: protection and security. **Negative:** locked up, inaccessible. **Also:** reforming the surface of the earth, creating lasting values, productivity, building up. A sign of patient hard work (see the bull below).

The bull – ❸

An old symbol for the earth (earth mother) in its fertility, but also as an awe-inspiring natural power (bullfight). In astrology, Taurus = the month of May: The merry month of May—renewal of the king's task in life!

The blackness – ❹

The primeval power of nature, of matter: epitome of all yet unresolved concerns, difficulties or darker aspects of life. At the same time the innards of the earth, its treasures, hitherto unexploited possibilities.

The foot on the stone – ❺

"Replenish the earth, and subdue it." **Positive:** the earth as homeland and dominion. **Negative:** misuse and destruction of natural reserves and the atmosphere.

The blue mountains / Clouds

Man's will is his *kingdom of heaven*. Blue clouds, or the blue mountains as well (as the link between heaven and earth). Life's spiritual dimension and that of the will form the background to the image.

The long, flowing robe – ❻

Positive: growing up with the throne and garden / vineyard. **Negative:** an overbearing person who disregards limits, lacks awareness. Warning against losing oneself in too much detail instead of showing a clear profile.

At the figure's back

The blue clouds / mountains and the castle lie behind the figure. One must consciously be aware of and deal with one's greater potential, what one is in the process of creating, one's own spiritual contribution.

KING OF PENTACLES / COINS

You are like this king. The card emphasizes your royal dignity and also your masculine attributes! You develop a majestic and appreciative way of dealing with the earth forces. All your capacities as a human being of great productivity, skill and sensibility are needed.

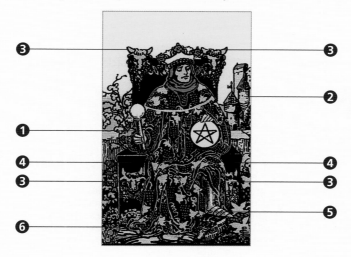

The vineyard and the grapes of life…

■ Basic meaning

The master of possessions: "What do I possess and how much? What are my capabilities? What is of permanent value?" As is the case with all the court cards, this king represents an ideal, the perfect mastery over the element in question, in this case the Pentacles (earth, material, money, talent, the physical). You are like this king—or you are well on your way! And/or you are destined to meet somebody who personifies this *king*.

■ Spiritual experience

The production, construction, and/or establishment of something that lives on into the future.

■ As the card for the day

Get your finances sorted out. Which talents can help you? Are there still some wishes remaining to be fulfilled after a productive life?

■ As a prognosis / tendency

You are your own capital—arable land and its harvest, the vineyard and its wine.

■ For love and relationships

Don't let yourself get bottled up! Be or become aware of your priceless value. Express your needs and undertake what is necessary for their fulfillment.

■ For success and happiness

Avoid letting your self-esteem be dependent on your money or the opinion of the world.

The 10 most important symbols

The card as a mirror

"The horse makes dung in its stable, and with great effort that horse hauls its dung to the field; and on the dung grows fine and noble wheat, which would never have been, were it not for the dung." (J. Tauler)

The black horse

The figure of the knight is made up of rider and horse together! Horse = instinctive nature and drives = one of the knight's aspects. Black can stand for the garbage of the past as well as for the unknown future.

The contrast of black and yellow

A strong contrast: The task of dealing with major personal contradictions so that they become productive. Seeing oneself as a field to be tilled and bringing order into one's personal affairs.

The armor – ❶

Positive: one is prepared —one experiences and provides protection and security. **Negative:** one remains a prisoner of one's own convictions, inflexibly insisting on something or some vision.

The arable land – ❷

Fruitfulness, being down-to-earth. The field of life, the field of experience. The task of working on oneself and tilling one's own acre. Sometimes also a warning against too much plowing through.

Green plumes – ❸

He who plows his own field and is not afraid of stark contradictions (black-yellow) will achieve and reap much in life. **Also:** back to nature—and a warning against immaturity.

The Pentacle and the sky

have the same hue. The pentacle is only distinguishable on account of its contour. Only experience and testing one's own limits (!) enable us to distinguish our own talents. The task of setting one's own limits.

The color yellow

Common consciousness, the sun—but also the search for meaning and envy, gold, and greed. The need to differentiate between the common consciousness and one's own, personal pentacle.

The red bridle – ❹

Red stands for the will, *joie-de-vivre* and passion, but also for covetousness and egoism. An invitation to put all one's enthusiasm into finding out what is one's own and exploring new territories.

Gauntlet / Saddle blanket – ❺

Only this knight is wearing gauntlets and has a blanket with him. **Positive:** prepared for work and cold weather. **Negative:** not prepared to get one's hands dirty, having something to cover up.

KNIGHT OF PENTACLES / COINS

KNIGHT OF PENTACLES

You are like this knight. The card emphasizes your sovereignty and also your masculine attributes! You have and are developing a masterful and holistic way of dealing with the earth forces of life. All your abilities as a human being of great experience, thoroughness and economic sense are needed.

The field of experience, treasures of the soil.

■ Basic meaning

The master of well-being and achievement: "What do I bring with me? What can I do well? What does me good?" As is the case with all the court cards, this knight represents an ideal, the perfect mastery over the element in question, in this case the Pentacles (earth, material, money, talent, the physical). You are like this knight—or you are well on your way! And/or you are destined to meet somebody who personifies this *knight*.

■ Spiritual experience

Ripening, completion, bringing in the crops—and the many steps, paths, and diversions to be taken on the way to reaping the harvest.

■ As the card for the day

Nothing gets wasted—even our waste products, personal and otherwise, can be fertilizer for the next cycle. Forgive yourself and others for not being perfect.

■ As a prognosis/tendency

By working steadily through things that need to get done, you develop experience and self-possesion.

■ For love and relationships

Don't try to avoid conflicts when they're due—on the contrary, seek them! You have the capabilities you need to solve problems.

■ For success and happiness

You can't change your fellow beings, but you can accept them in a way that allows their abilities to shine.

The 10 most important symbols

The figure's position or pose

 He appears to be carefully checking whether the pentacle (coin) is genuine. Or seeing it as a fragile wonder, holding it almost as if it were a delicate bubble – a scene of ethereal lightness.

The position of the hands – ❶

 Positive: great reverence, careful treatment of valuables and talents, not least with one's own self-esteem, talents and tasks. **Negative:** being over-careful, not really grasping the essentials.

The color yellow

 The Sun, but also sensual longing and envy, gold and greed. **Danger:** getting too close to the sun can provoke a fall (into fantasy or delusion). **Positive:** the hidden side is lit up too = reliable subconscious.

The Pentacle and the sky – ❷

 have the same hue. The pentacle is only distinguishable on account of its contour. Only experience and testing one's own limits enable us to distinguish our own talents. The task of setting one's own limits.

The meadow landscape – ❸

 The blue mountains, the piece of arable land and the multitude of meadow flowers stand for the treasures waiting to be discovered. They are like the gold which, according to the old adage, paves the streets.

The trees – ❹

 In the image for *the Knight of Pentacles* two trees are standing at the edge; here we see a clump. **Positive:** variety, keeping together, community. **Negative:** overmuch need to belong, too much or too little self-will.

The blue mountains – ❺

 The peak stands for the link between heaven and earth. Generally, blue is the color of the sky, so the blue of the mountains once again heralds the marriage between heaven and earth.

The arable land

 Symbol for the field of life, the field of experience. Task: to work on oneself. "What do you want to reap?"

The color green

 Positive: growth, nature, naturalness, freshness, hope, gradual growth. **Negative:** much immaturity, false hopes (idealism), not fully developed, greenhorn.

The red headgear – ❻

 Positive: will, eagerness, passion, 'heart' and emotionalism. **Warning:** arrogance, hothead. **Encouragement:** pride, self-confidence, curiosity, visions.

PAGE OF PENTACLES

You are like this page. The card emphasizes your sovereignty and also your young and youthful attributes! You develop a masterly, innovative way of dealing with the earth forces. All your skills as a human being of great humor and instinct are needed.

Keep a hold on what is fruitful and valuable!

■ Basic meaning

The adventure of discovery and the search: "What is available? What can be made of it?" As is the case with all the court cards, this page represents an ideal, the perfect mastery over the element in question, in this case the Pentacles (earth, material, money, talent, the physical). You are like this page—or you are well on your way! And/or you are destined to meet somebody who personifies this *page*.

■ Spiritual experience

Being productive. Finding something. Planting something. Having an effect beyond oneself.

■ As the card for the day

Make today an adventure full of new discoveries!

■ As a prognosis / tendency

The pentacle is a gift of life. And a mirror to show that you are a treasure for yourself and for your surroundings as soon as you grasp your talents.

■ For love and relationships

Loving someone also means making demands on his/her talents!

■ For success and happiness

Our talents are often like the gold that, as the saying goes, paves the streets. At first they seem as inconspicuous as a yellow coin on a yellow backdrop.

The 10 most important symbols

The card as a mirror

You are like a coin with two aspects—a shining side and a shadowy one. What sort of mold formed you? And the flip side: What is it that you are going to mold and form?

Pentagram – ❶

An ancient magic symbol. The vibration of energy (the atoms) in the earth. A representation of the human figure (the points indicating the hands, feet and head). The four elements and their culmination in the *quintessence.*

The double edge – ❷

The image manages to convey a reference to the proverbial two sides of a coin by means of the double rim: positive and negative impressions, aptitudes and handicaps, as well as many other opposites.

The Pentacles I

Pentacle = earth element: all that is material, both in the sense of financial and material value as well as matter, the physical (mother, matrix). The pentacles/coins have to do with practical tasks and results.

The Pentacles II

Keywords for the pentacles: material values and talents. Money and validity. And talents in the sense of personal faculties and tasks waiting to be discovered and realized.

The hand emerging from a cloud / corona – ❸

The Pentacle is a gift to you. You, yourself, are a gift—for yourself and for the world. Accept this gift and make something of it. Take it in your hands and let it multiply.

The gray sky

Gray is associated with being unruffled, self-possessed. **Positive:** lack of bias, neutrality, patience. **Negative:** lack of awareness, indifference. All this in respect to the value and usefulness of your talent.

The garden / white lilies – ❹

The world as a place to live, cultivated earth. White—the color for beginnings and completion. The garden of childhood, the human paradise that we have left behind and to which we seek to return.

The blue mountains – ❺

The peak stands for the connecting link between heaven and earth—blue is also the color of the sky. **And:** "Make something out your talents!" Climb your mountain, allow something beneficial to emerge from your potential!

The garden gate – ❻

The borderline between reality and the other world. **A recurring experience:** crossing a threshold, embarking on a new stage in life. Departing in order to arrive. Paradise lost and paradise regained!

ACE OF PENTACLES / COINS

ACE OF PENTACLES

The Pentacle symbolizes talent and wealth—material, financial, physical. The Pentacles are the embodiment of nature and culture. They are our heritage, containing in them not yet completed tasks and not yet exploited possibilities. The blue mountains and the garden are further references to this potential.

Praise be to that which helps us appreciate and enjoy life!

■ Basic meaning

The Pentacles express our talents and personal wealth: one side of the coin concerns our stamp in the sense of our characteristics that each of us has brought with us—both capacities and impediments. All together, these constitute a person's talents. When we accept them, work on them, and fashion something new with them, we, the created, become creators as well—of our circumstances and of the traces which we leave behind. The Cups are the vessels which give our feelings, spiritual needs, longings and beliefs a home. The essential thing is *flow* and the purification of the soul with water. The Ace provides an elementary way in. It's all yours!

■ Spiritual experience

Recognizing one's task, calling, gifts—as one's fate and chance!

■ As the card for the day

Get your talents rolling. Do your own thing!

■ As a prognosis / tendency

We think that only experts have talent. In fact, we all do. Each one of us is uniquely good at something.

■ For love and relationships

Loving means saying "Yes!" to someone, in all her/his uniqueness and potential.

■ For success and happiness

It is yours—as task and opportunity—to define the circumstances of your life, weigh up the significance of your existence—and then to dare.

The 10 most important symbols

The two Pentacles I

stand for the proverbial two sides of the coin: In different ways, all our personal strengths and shortcomings, bright sides and seamy sides, gifts and disabilities have something to do with each other...

The two Pentacles II

...and need to be sorted out (so that strengths and weaknesses are not mistaken for each other, for instance). But this does not mean tearing them apart (hence the green band)—both aspects together are what makes the man.

The green band / the horizontal eight – ❶

Positive: the endless possibilities, one's personal contribution to the cosmic game, intactness, wholeness. **Negative:** humdrum routine, treadmill, repetition (running in a circle).

The sailing ships I – ❷

"...that the most excellent person must needs have adverse qualities also, like as a great ship in full sail, which needeth ballast, that its weight be sufficient for a proper passage." (Gottfried Keller)

The sailing ships II

The sailing ship is also a symbol for the ability to handle the changing winds of fortune so skillfully as to be able to reach a safe harbor in any conditions. **Warning:** don't sail too close to the wind.

The waves – ❸

Life's high points and low points. Personal growth. Passage to new continents. All life began in the oceans: this brings to mind our origins, our personal part in creation.

Green band / green shoes – ❹

Green is the color of life, vitality, growth and therefore also of hope. But on the other hand it can stand for immaturity, lack of finish, something being half baked.

The color of the clothing

Red stands for the will and passion, but also eagerness, sometimes over eagerness. The color of the tunic represents a mixture of the red with the yellow of the pentacles—the will and sun, or eagerness with envy and greed.

The large hat – ❺

The large red hat, like a rooster's comb, suggests ego, too much zeal, haughtiness (especially insofar as the figure is unaware of what is going on behind him). **Positive:** a crown, growing beyond oneself, an accolade.

The hem of the tunic – ❻

An unusual pattern (only to be seen on this card): perhaps a fear of being *hemmed in?* **Positive:** when you turn to face the contradictions in your life, they can appear as an interesting decoration!

Two of Pentacles

Coming to terms with contradictions: personal strengths and weaknesses, one's own and other people's problems, the principles of pleasure and duty at odds with each other, the sunny and the seamy sides. You, too, are like a coin: You have your stamp, you set your stamp on the world.

The two sides of the coin…

■ Basic meaning

A sea change. A shift in life's focus. New facts, values, and results come to the foreground in your present situation and present you with a new perspective. Something, some possibility that was waiting in the wings, comes forward and takes on new meaning. Don't try to play dice with fate, and don't dig your heels in either. The solution is to come to grips with the contradictions. You already have what you need in your hands to juggle all the elements into a favorable position.

■ Spiritual experience

You bring new facts into the world and that way you help to form the face of the earth.

■ As the card for the day

You need (and find) new results.

■ As a prognosis/tendency

You may reckon with temporary upsets and a degree of insecurity when your life undergoes change. How else can you get around to casting off old habits and developing into a new state of consciousness?

■ For love and relationships

"It is indeed curious that the most excellent person must needs have adverse qualities also,…

■ For success and happiness

…like as a great ship in full sail, which needeth ballast, that its weight be sufficient for a proper passage." (Gottfried Keller)

The 10 most important symbols

The image as a mirror

Only this card shows *black* pentacles. **A warning** against characters who resemble voles and moles. **Encouragement:** to delve deeply, find buried treasure and reveal new ways. Find yourself and come out into the open!

The sculptor / mason – ❶

A chisel in the left hand, a mallet in the right. He is working on the stone, perhaps a relief. Michelangelo pointed out that in his work he put nothing into the stone, but instead he simply freed…

The unhewn stone – ❷

…the sculpture already present from the ballast surrounding it. The unhewn stone is man with his potential and his slag; with his calling that still slumbers within him!

The crypt / the cellar

Here we have to do with foundations, basic values, groundwork in the sphere of the Pentacles (money, values, talents). On the basis of these vaults a mighty construction will rise up: How will your work contribute to it?

The black Pentacles I – ❸

Black Pentacles/coins: either personal needs, finances, and talents remain misjudged, forgotten or ignored. Or they have simply not yet become exposed, not yet been recognized: latent talents!

The black Pentacles II

Negative: "To possess a talent and fail to use it means to misuse it." (Duke Clemens August of Weimar) **Positive:** you bring light into the darkness. You are not afraid of an encounter with the unknown.

The monk – ❹

Basic values and peak performance: having a vocation can lead to great achievements, because one is more committed. Membership of an order = living one's calling. **And:** every true calling also has its spiritual side.

Nun / fool / noblewoman – ❺

As nun = vocation, as with the monk next to her. **As a fool,** the figure underlines the aspects of freedom and the absolute. **As a noblewoman =** beauty and importance of personal values and basic tenets.

The twofold plan –

The figures on the right are holding two copies of a plan, a sketch or a drawing. These have to do with career-related projects. **Spiritual:** the blueprint of creation—what God has in store for you.

The bench

The *Eight of Pentacles* and this card both show a man with a hammer and chisel as well as a bench. Here, its purpose is to elevate (uplift, lift a ban etc.) a person in his work and through his work.

THREE OF PENTACLES

Various aspects of work, profession and vocation are to be seen: working with materials, re-forming the earth, working on oneself, the disclosure of what was hidden. Also, working with others and for others. What contribution does one's own work make?

Positive: The hidden side is lit up too = reliable subconscious.

■ Basic meaning

Only on this card are the pentacles depicted in black. Either the personal needs, finances, and talents are ignored, or they are as yet undeveloped, unnamed. This is about your own calling: Go deeper! One's vocation helps one up to great heights because one recognizes what lies hidden—just as the genius Michelangelo remarked that the sculptor adds nothing to the stone, but simply liberates the figure shut up within it from its encumbrances.

■ Spiritual experience

A true vocation is a great and joyful passion...

■ As the card for the day

Everyone has summits that are waiting for him or her...

■ As a prognosis / tendency

... of varying heights, of course. But *every* single mountain has a peak. The crucial question remains as to whether you will reach *your* particular peak.

■ For love and relationships

Don't just ask what you want for yourself; find out what God and the world want from you—then your path will be all the easier and more worthwhile!

■ For success and happiness

Find that task which develops and sculpts your abilities best.

The 10 most important symbols

The figure's position or pose

The figure appears to be stooping somewhat, a warning against false humility and a cramped attitude (crooked back). Still, with the pentacle above his head he is by no means small, but rather grand.

The thing itself I – ❶

The figure clearly has a thing about pentacles—the feet resting on two, one above his head and another clasped in front of his breast. **Negative:** an anxious zealot who blames the circumstances…

The thing itself II

…**Positive:** a master of his trade who has learned his métier to perfection, become one with it. New discoveries demand personal soul-searching at all levels.

The crown – ❷

Negative: egoism, boastfulness. One thinks one is the king. **Positive:** one is a king. A real pro. A master of one's own realm, of successful utilization of values and talents.

The towers / the city – ❸

The many towers are reminiscent of towns in Tuscany. Towers stand for watchfulness, protection, safety, justified pride and might, but also detachment, captivity, isolation, megalomania.

The town at the figure's back

It is good to turn away from the crowd in order to be able to hone one's own talents and develop one's professionalism. On the other hand—who benefits? Make your own specific contribution, throw in your capacities—and yourself!

The black mantle – ❹

The black is an echo of the motives of the *Three of Pentacles:* unknown talents waiting for the light of day. True expertise includes the ability to discover something new in old patterns. A **warning** against living like a mole!

The eggplant-colored robe – ❺

An unusual color in this tarot, an allusion to the sphere of digestion and feces. **Negative:** anal fixation (Sigmund Freud). **Positive:** the ability to turn muck into money.

The stone block – ❻

A symbol of the material, the earth with the four points of the compass. The task and the art of finding one's place in the world. *IV-The Emperor* on the level of the Pentacles: self-determination in a material and practical sense.

The gray sky

A **warning** against lack of awareness, emotional indifference, lack of involvement (including lack of concern about one's own needs and wishes). **Positive:** lack of bias, neutrality, lack of prejudice.

FOUR OF PENTACLES

A professional from top to toe: Paying regard to the two pentacles below, results in a grounded, but flat life. Taking the middle pentacle to heart raises the plane of life to that which can be grasped. And the master who can crown himself with the upper pentacle has found out how to use all his talents to the full.

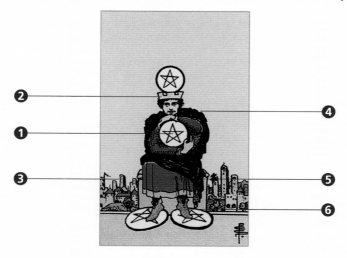

"To possess a talent and fail to use it means to misuse it."

■ Basic meaning

The ability to grasp and crown oneself with one's own talents demands both that one sets oneself apart from the world and that one enters into its service. If we wish neither to become outsiders, nor for our special qualities to get sucked under in the crowd, we need to establish exactly what talents we have that can be useful and important for others and make the best use of our own experience and knowledge.

■ Spiritual experience

An intimate interrelationship between the person and the material world.

■ As the card for the day

Develop your ability and what matters to you. And see what's waiting to be discovered at your feet!

■ As a prognosis / tendency

Sometimes this card is a reminder that it is time to withdraw and do one's own thing. And sometimes to open up and be more communicative.

■ For love and relationships

Among other things, love means helping each other to establish a personal sphere of influence—and to occupy that sphere as its rightful sovereign!

■ For success and happiness

Neither bragging nor fawning will get you ahead, but rather patiently cultivating your best talents.

The 10 most important symbols

The card as a mirror

This card is certainly not automatically one of need and misfortune—it is also a lucky one, in that it stands (among other things) for overcoming hardship of all kinds and for the wholeness of all that we hold dear.

The blind and lame persons I

The old story of the blind man and lame man who pooled their resources fits exactly into this scene. United we stand —and the worst of the difficulties are solved.

Relieving the need

The blindness and lameness represent any kind of disability or problem. The greatest need is eased. So the general message of the card is: Address *your* needs, take account of what you *need*.

The blind and lame persons II

The main significance is to be found in their cooperation. As a supplement: acceptance of our differences. Each may develop and seek fulfillment in his or her own way.

The crutches – ❶

On the one hand a graphic accentuation of the difficult situation, of the need that is present or has already been overcome. But the crutches are also a sign that there is a solution to the problem, aid and support are available.

The plague bell – ❷

Outcasts had to carry such a bell to warn other people of the danger of infection. **But the bell also has a positive aspect:** Here I am, an exceptional person. Every crisis is also an opportunity.

The white ground – ❸

Obvious: snow, ice, and cold. **Positive:** reminder of the need to clarify something, to get things cleared, healed, and restored between yourself and others or just for yourself. A **warning** against groundless (mis-)behavior.

Snowflakes / black wall – ❹

Obvious: snow, ice and cold. Also **symbolic** for blurred contrast between black and white, walls becoming permeable, transparent: inside and outside are two sides of the same coin.

Light shines into the darkness – ❺

Light, warmth, wealth on the one side, darkness, cold, poverty on the other. It is a matter of involvement and accepting a share of the responsibility, of people's predicaments within and without, and of yours.

Five Pentacles as the quintessence

The greatest talents are only of any use if they bring benefit to others, and where the need is greatest, the help and support is most valuable. Helping others and helping oneself as a complementary pair.

FIVE OF PENTACLES

A scene of destitution. But also how it can be overcome: Legend tells of a blind person and a cripple who joined forces and gave each other what support they could—the blind man helped the lame one along; the cripple guided the blind man. Sharing their needs and abilities relieved their hardship.

Needs must when the devil drives!

■ Basic meaning
Every human capacity (possessions and abilities) has a value equal to the extent to which it is used to prevent hardship from occurring and to ease it when it is unavoidable. Some states of distress arise through *force majeur*—an act of God—while others come from unfulfilled needs: the need to make sense of life, a thirst for love, yearning for home. Where all your potential is devoted to the relief of the most dire problems, that is where your talents are most effective.

■ Spiritual experience
"Let God share in your lack. He has none." (Dorothee Sölle)

■ As the card for the day
The capacities of one who works alone add up. Those of a person who cooperates with others are multiplied.

■ As a prognosis / tendency
Sometimes it's the right time to throw in the towel, accept defeat, come to terms with a lack. But the fact remains that there is much unnecessary need and unhappiness in the world—and in yourself. It is well worth undertaking something against it.

■ For love and relationships
Reject unjustified claims and pointless sacrifice.

■ For success and happiness
Fulfill worthwhile duties with a light heart!

The 10 most important symbols

The card as a mirror

Without thinking about it beforehand: in which of the three figures do you immediately see yourself? All three, together or individually, could be a mirror of your personality. Compare also *V - The Hierophant*.

The rich man – ❶

The large figure stands for your strengths, wealth of experience, and talents—your faculties, which are always there and of which you have enough to be able to share. Never mind how your bank balance looks right now.

The two supplicants – ❷

stand for one's own weaknesses. One of them receives alms, the other nothing. These two beggars, too, are important parts of your personality and an expression of valuable experience.

The scales I – ❸

The scales as an image for weighing up the pros and cons: which requests are sensible and should be granted, which are futile and should be refused? Consider carefully what needs are important to you.

The scales II

When give and take are balanced out, there are two possible—and contrasting—reasons: either that which was taken and that which was given are trifling, have no weight. Or we have a win-win situation.

The four small coins I – ❹

When the giver, while giving, feels enriched instead of losing something, and when the recipient, while receiving, feels substantiated in his value as a human being instead of feeling ashamed...

The four small coins II

...then added value is generated, because both sides feel richer than they did before. This added value is represented by the four small coins that form the link between the giving and receiving hands.

The sign of blessing – ❺

The fingers of the rich man repeat the gesture of *The Hierophant*. **Positive:** there is indeed something hallowed about this win-win situation. **Negative:** arrogance, moralizing, welfare handout.

The Pentacles in the sky – ❻

Negative: true prosperity fails to reach the people down below. **Positive:** where giving and taking form a genuinely harmonious balance we create a little piece of heaven on earth.

The city / the castle – ❼

lies some distance in the background. One needs to detach oneself from the busy routine and bustle in order to come to terms with oneself and one's strengths and weaknesses. **Negative:** stewing in one's own juice.

Six of Pentacles

This card is about give and take, dealing with needs, with the turnover of talents. When talents are put to optimal use, then those who possess them and those who benefit from them have equal advantages.

A win-win situation?

■ **Basic meaning**

Charity, welfare? This is about more than that. When your talents help to relieve need and your needs help to awaken talents, then the net result is positive for all—the classic win-win situation. That way, necessities and neediness can be transformed into creative and genuinely consecrated activity. This added extra is indicated by the four small coins in the image.

■ **Spiritual experience**

The value of what is one's own is greatest when as many people as possible can profit from it. In that sense you only possess what you give away.

■ **As the card for the day**

Today's agenda contains new ways of realizing your own wishes and satisfying those of others.

■ **As a prognosis / tendency**

Concentrate on creating added value for all those involved. That's a great deal better than spending your time patching up the deficiencies.

■ **For love and relationships**

Give and take: you create a situation in which it is perfectly OK to take and receive, ...

■ **For success and happiness**

...in which you can dare to be weak without provoking harshness or hostility.

The 10 most important symbols

The figure's position or pose I

Waiting, musing, taking a break or coming to a halt. Whether your work lies ahead of you or behind you, the situation here has to do with taking stock or perhaps solving a mystery: "What's the meaning of all this?"

The figure's position or pose II

Has he no idea which way to turn?! Or perhaps he is just having a creative pause. Or carefully checking over what is there, searching for signs and traces!

The distribution of the Pentacles I – ❶

The heap of pentacles shows how things have always been done so far, in the regular way. The single one at his/your feet marks the new approach, your own standpoint, the innovation.

The different colors of the boots – ❷

If instead of assessing the situation—what needs to be done—from one's own, personal point of view one only takes general considerations into account—then the boot is indeed on the other foot!

The distribution of the Pentacles II

There are, as the saying goes, two sides to everything. Some aspects only become clear when one is prepared to question one's own standpoint and see things from a different perspective.

The expression I – ❸

The position of the head expresses tiredness or perplexity, but also careful study. The origin of the word 'religion' is thought to be 're-reading'—thorough investigation.

The expression II

He who takes all aspects of a situation into careful consideration may need more time than others. But he is more likely to find hidden interrelationships and new solutions.

The hoe I – ❹

An ell, a yardstick. Symbolic of the proper implementation of the right tool, for effective correlation between mind and matter (for which every pentacle with its inscribed pentagram stands generally).

The hoe II

Experience already gained = a tool for creating something new. Pick out what is valid from traditional ways, add your own contribution and let the existing positive approaches work together and create something new.

The mixed colors – ❺

of the clothing show: what is one's own and what comes from outside, tradition and one's own point of view, are intermingled. You will now find the task that suits you—the contribution that the world has been waiting for!

SEVEN OF PENTACLES

You may have a mountain of effort and difficulties behind you or in front of you; at this point it is a question of appraising your results to date and determining new targets. Are you satisfied with your results? How you have worked? Subject your results to a thorough investigation.

What's the meaning of all this?

■ **Basic meaning**

All things and tasks have, in addition to their purely factual aspects, a *personal significance* as well. What are you proud of? Is there something that bugs you? Something missing? Find out where you see things differently to others. What would you most like to do away with? What do you want to plant? What habits do you want to cultivate?

■ **Spiritual experience**

In order to see where you stand, you need to take stock—again and again. This careful, dedicated process of observation is what the word religion basically means (Latin: re-connection, but also 're-consideration').

■ **As the card for the day**

Consider your current questions and search for signs and traces. Sometimes even stumbling blocks can provide useful hints.

■ **As a prognosis / tendency**

Time to take stock: the value of emotional or mental clarity depends on your ability to reap useful results. And your achievements only bring you satisfaction to the extent to which you can identify yourself with them.

■ **For love and relationships**

What would you like to cultivate, to grow, and then give to your dearest and to the world?

■ **For success and happiness**

Stick to what is genuine.

The 10 most important symbols

The figure's position or pose

This is the only card in this suit in which the figure in the image is actually working on the pentacles. A picture of a craftsman at work: at work on a task or an object, but also a metaphor for working on oneself.

Working on the Pentacle I – ❶

No mastery can be achieved without learning and practice. If the figure still has to work on another seven pentacles, he appears as an apprentice. But if work on the other seven is finished, then he appears as the master.

Working on the Pentacle II

Like a coin, every person has some traits that seem to jut out, and some that seem rather plain/plane. **One side of the coin is concerned with:** what has molded me? **And the other side:** what am I going to mold?

Pole with Pentacles – ❷

Positive: moderation marks the true master. Here restricting oneself to a single skill so as not to become jack-of-all-trades and master of none. Connection between heaven and earth. **Negative:** monotony, repetition.

One Pentacle on the ground – ❸

This pentacle emphasizes one's own situation, one's personal distinction, perhaps also a new approach —but also a pentacle that falls by the wayside, i.e., strengths and talents that are not given enough attention.

Blue and red

The colors of fire and water: when appearing together they stand for zeal and passion. **Positive:** great willingness to put in effort, overcoming difficulties. **Negative:** blind dedication, repetitiveness.

The village in the background

Note: at the figure's back. Getting away from the crowd in order to be able to develop the particular strengths of one's own talents. But the greatest talents remain worthless if they do not contribute to the benefit of others.

The bench – ❹

Positive: be your own benchmark. Do it yourself. Do what needs doing and use/work on your talents. **Negative:** lack of confidence in others. Tendency to pay too much attention to detail.

Markings on the pole – ❺

Positive: annual rings, patience, growth, mastery, gradual development. **Negative:** knotholes, lack of alternative (branches), empty routine, repetition complex, lack of imagination, boredom.

Hammer and chisel – ❻

Positive: an image of one's own ability to make an impression. The ability to create sustainable value. Change and lasting values. **Negative:** need to put one's own stamp on everyone and everything.

EIGHT OF PENTACLES / COINS

EIGHT OF PENTACLES

The range of Pentacles stands for experience and mastery, but also for lack of imagination and monotony. Mastery means that one's work doesn't just use energy, but returns it as well. Also: that one finds one's own style and a creative dialog between oneself and one's métier.

Master of Arts…

■ Basic meaning

We are like coins: we have been forged in God's furnace and we ourselves create an impression. So the work on the pentacles is a mirror of our work on ourselves. The productivity of a person consists in his abilities to produce himself and to produce order in the things of his world. Thus you develop a situation of personal luxury: a wealth of well-being, ideas that have become reality and fulfilled wishes. All aspects are important—not just the end results, but also the accompanying circumstances.

■ Spiritual experience

Gurus produce pupils. Only (one's own) practice makes the perfect master.

■ As the card for the day

Don't let yourself be used up for somebody else's benefit: search out what is really important to you!

■ As a prognosis / tendency

The master is the true beginner. Precisely his own skill shows him that all his previous experience is history.

■ For love and relationships

Love is not just a question of feelings, but also of mutual support in realizing each partner's life's work.

■ For success and happiness

You are, and you remain the boss in your life. Even if you aren't self-employed. You are the leader and the master of your life, director of your life's work, steady and firm.

The 10 most important symbols

The robe

The scene is one of splendor, beauty, and expensive finery. But the long train could also provoke doubts: Is the robe overlarge for its wearer? Or is he dragging his past about with him?

The hedge

Is the figure in the picture in front of the hedge (from your point of view) or behind it (from the point of view of the rest of the world)? Is the display of talent radiating into the world, or being kept hidden away?

The falcon – ❶

Cultivated hunting or aggressive egoism? The falcon is wearing a hood, so it is quiet, but ready for action. Is that concentrating resources or frustratingly limiting? Mighty passion or just blind instinct?

The snail – ❷

Positive: the snail feels at home everywhere. It can always find somewhere to withdraw. It is independent of others, has its own rhythm. **Negative:** a painfully slow pace, escape from reality, lack of involvement.

The distribution of the Pentacles – ❸

The theme of the *Six of Pentacles:* Give and take —the use and expression of personal abilities and needs. As with the *Three of Pentacles:* promotion and development of hidden talents.

The grapes I – ❹

Grapes and wine = sublime enjoyment: the sensory pleasures and joys of sensuality (Dionysian, the wine god Bacchus or Dionysos) and taking pleasure in the pursuit of meaning and truth (Apollonian; *in vino veritas*).

The grapes II

From time immemorial grapes have also symbolized gruelingly hard work—the laborers in the vineyard provide a lasting image of what it means to earn one's living with the sweat of one's brow.

The grapes III

As grapes are among the fruits that ripen latest of all; they also symbolize maturity, success in life, and fulfillment (see also *Ten of Pentacles:* the old man with the grapes).

The flowers on the robe – ❺

Flower power. A blooming personality. A variant of the sign of Venus. Symbol for the fertility of (one's own) nature. **Negative:** narcissistic, concerned only with oneself. **Positive:** using one's talents to the best.

The small house at the edge of the image – ❻

Positive: surrounded by the coins, i.e., one's talents and the fruits arising from them, one finds where one truly belongs. **Negative:** underdeveloped identity, a child of nature, a loner.

NINE OF PENTACLES

You come into bloom: you reach a state of personal prosperity (at any age) and can take pleasure in your existence and to be satisfied with your talents. You harvest their fruits day by day with loving awareness of your situation and with your devotion. Be pleased with yourself, and how you ripen more and more!

Manifold talents!

■ Basic meaning

It makes a huge difference that you are living in the world. You have something which makes it a richer place, so don't hide your talents under a bushel! Be generous; show your fellow human beings what treasures you have in store—because you, yourself, are priceless.

■ Spiritual experience

The rose bush can only develop its beauty through the cut: with determination you dispense with irrelevant ideals, undesired obligations, and *laissez-faire* experiments.

■ As the card for the day

Stop flying around like a restless falcon all the time—or withdrawing into your shell all the time.

■ As a prognosis / tendency

There is much in the world that is completely indifferent to who we are, and by no means do we always find a loving welcome. And our response is fed from our own bounteous store of love, fruitfulness and beauty!

■ For love and relationships

Rise above pettiness and jealousy.

■ For success and happiness

Distance yourself from pointless habits and routines. Make up rules according to your own wisdom—and abide by them!

The 10 most important symbols

The 10 Sephirot – ❶

The ten pentacles mark the stations of the cabalistic tree of life (10 Sephirot). However, there are no lines joining these ten corner points. That means: everything is there, but the connections are missing.

The generations –

Childhood, midlife, and age are all to be seen. Are they aware of each other? Or do they live their lives in separate worlds? The two figures standing in the center: Are they involved with each other in some way or simply passersby?

Man and animal – ❸

The same question concerns mankind and the animal kingdom. Are our animal aspects beyond the pale? How much do we understand the might of nature and instincts, their strengths and weaknesses?

Culture—nature – ❹

Wavy lines on the left = lake or sea. **Houses under the arch =** civilization. Is there an intrinsic link between nature and culture, or does the one exist only through suppression of the other?

Old man with grapes – ❺

Grapes = enjoyment and hard work (vineyard). At the same time a ripe old age: "Anyone who imagines that all fruits ripen with the strawberries knows nothing about grapes." (Paracelsus)

Staff / Spear – ❻

Positive: the envisaged goal has been reached, the staff has done its job. **But also:** remain prepared, stay alert. **Negative:** always under way: knocking on every door and not really at home anywhere.

Bridge – ❼

Love, respect, and appreciation form the bridge that links person to person. Everything is there, but is there any inner relation or tie? And the bridge is only half visible.

Castle / tower

Positive: attentiveness, alertness, an overview, protection, definite identity, home, security. **Negative:** ivory tower, egoism, arrogance, captivity, isolation, self-restriction, reticence.

Two coats of arms – ❽

Castle: see above—**The balanced scales** (cf. *Six of Pentacles):* No flow, no exchange, nothing of any weight. **Or on the positive side:** Giving and receiving are of equal value. Balancing needs.

Odysseus / end of the odyssey

At the end of his wanderings Odysseus returns to Thebes. He disguises himself as a beggar, recognizable only to his dogs, and then makes a clean sweep. What is there in your life waiting to be addressed and sorted out?

TEN OF PENTACLES

Child, adult, old man; man and animal; culture and civilization, home and foreign parts—and much more: It is all there, and the only question is, is there any connection between the elements (see bridge), or do they simply go past each other (perhaps as people pass by the beggar at the gate)?!

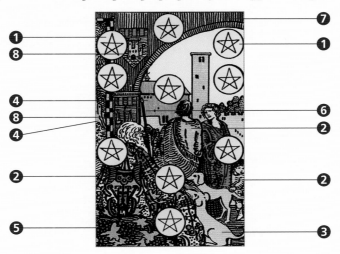

No man is an island…

■ Basic meaning

The greatest riches consist in / result from becoming aware of one's own part in the affairs of the world. Your experiences and those of others mingle to form a greater whole. You see yourself as part of creation, of the cosmic flow. You know that your deeds build on the foundation laid by those who have gone before and they will be continued by your successors. Time is only relative. Nothing is wasted. Nothing can prevent you from living and feeling your pulse, tarrying and then taking your leave.

■ Spiritual experience

Time is only relative.

■ As the card for the day

Consciously take on the people and events of your life and accept them in love. The results will astound you.

■ As a prognosis / tendency

True, conscious individuality cannot be experienced in isolation. Loneliness, that shadow of a missing individuality, disappears when we find the bridge that links us to others—just as does the danger of being swallowed up by the crowd.

■ For love and relationships

Be actively 'pro-community' …

■ For success and happiness

… and work toward a coexistence in which everyone can find their own path and fulfillment.

The Top 10 Spreads

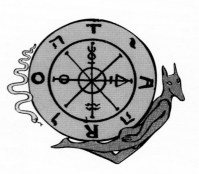

1 *Three cards for the day*

2	1	3

1 the situation
2 the task
3 the solution

2 *The oracle*

1	2	3

1 the present problem
2 the way out
3 the future—if you are prepared
to take that path

3 *A peek into the future—I*

2	1	3

1 the current situation
2 the past, or what is already there
3 the future, or something new to be taken
into account

4 *A peek into the future—II*

	5	
2	1	3
	4	

1 the key, or main aspect
2 the past, or what is already there
3 the future, or something new to be taken
into account
4 the root, or base
5 the crown, the opportunity, the trend

5 The way ahead

1	2	3	4

1 you already know / have this
2 you can do this well
3 this is new
4 this is what you can learn

6 The star

	1	
2	5	4
	3	

1 where you are standing now
2 your tasks
3 your difficulties or your reservations
4 your strengths
5 your goal

7 Living with uncertainty

		6		
	5		7	
1				8
	2		4	
		3		

1 this is possible
2 this is important
3 this is courageous
4 this is trivial
5 this is necessary
6 this is lighthearted
7 this is witty
8 this takes you farther

8 *The way*

1 | **1** This is what it's all about. These are the opportunities and the risks in relation to the question.

Left column = your behavior up to the present

2 | **7** | **2** Conscious attitudes, thoughts, rational grounds, ideas, intentions, modes of behavior of which the questioner is aware. Rational behavior.

3 | **6** | **3** Unconscious attitudes, wishes, longings which the questioner has in his or her heart. Hopes and fears. Emotional behavior.

4 | **5** | **4** Outward attitudes. How the questioner appears to his or her surroundings, perhaps also his or her façade.

Right column = suggestion for future behavior: the interpretations correspond to fields 2-4

7 Conscious attitude. Suggestion for a rational mode of action.

6 Unconscious attitude. Suggestion for one's emotional orientation.

5 Outward attitude. This is how the questioner should present himself/herself to the world.

© Hajo Banzhaf, *Das Arbeitsbuch zum Tarot*, München 1989

9 *The way of desires*

1 | **3** | **4** | **5** | **2**

1 the present situation
2 the desired goal
3, 4, 5 a bridge from **1** to **2**

With this spread, the cards are not drawn blind, but selected. First, choose an image, calmly and deliberately, which represents your present situation. Then look for one that shows what should, in your opinion, happen, i.e., what you wish for yourself. Take as much time as you need. Then pick out three additional cards that can be used as connecting links, as a bridge that will take you from the present situation to the goal that you wish to reach. Finally, look on the cards, in their entirety, as a complete path and story.

The Celtic cross (one possible variant)

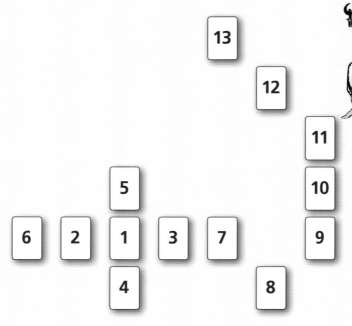

1   subject of the question—you, yourself
2   positive addition to **1**
3   negative addition to **1**
4   root, basis, support
5   crown, opportunity, trend
6   the past or what is already there
7   the future or something new to be taken into account
8   summary of the positions 1–7; your inner strength,
    your subconscious
9   hopes and fears
10   the environment and external influences; your role as seen by others
11, 12, 13 (draw 1–3 cards for this position as your intuition tells you)—a
    summary, or a point to which your attention is drawn especially—
    one which already exists and which will gain a special significance for
    your question.

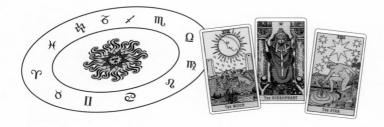

Tarot and Astrology

The origins of astrology reach back many thousands of years. In contrast, the cards of the tarot are much younger, even though their nearly 600 years can be seen as a ripe old age! Strangely, it was only as recently as the end of the nineteenth century that the connection between tarot and astrology became a subject of serious discussion in authoritative circles.

The essential groundwork needed to bring the two symbolic languages together was done by the **Order of the Golden Dawn.** This was a magical order founded in England by members of a Rosicrucian Society around the turn of the nineteenth century. The order elaborated the associations between the astrological symbols and those of the tarot that are still in regular use today.

The most commonly used tarot decks, namely the Rider / Waite Tarot and the Crowley-Thoth Tarot, were devised by people who had previously been adherents of the Golden Dawn order: Pamela Colman Smith and Arthur E. Waite (Rider / Waite Tarot) and Lady Frieda Harris und Aleister Crowley (Thoth Tarot). In designing the decks both artist / author pairs adhered, with minor exceptions, to the pattern of astrological associations already established by the Golden Dawn order.

Therefore many of the Rider / Waite cards reflect these associations directly within the image itself (e.g. the sign of Capricorn on the card *IV – The Emperor* and the bull's heads (Taurus) in the image of the *King of Pentacles* or Coins). In the Crowley deck these associations are almost exclusively indicated through the use of symbols.

How to connect Tarot and Astrology

Each sign of the zodiac and each planet has certain tarot cards assigned to them. Thus *The High Priestess* card stands for the astrological moon, i.e. the individual realm of the soul and the subconscious. And *The Moon* of the tarot belongs to Pisces as the epitome of the collective subconscious and the oceanic feelings.

The following table shows which six tarot cards are associated with each sign of the zodiac. Which astrological sign interests you most at the moment? Pick out the six corresponding cards from your tarot deck and consider them carefully. All six together form a collage that can be used to gain an understanding of the respective sign of the zodiac.

Examples:
Aries: Among the six cards we find a contradiction represented by *The Emperor* and *The Tower*, between consolidation and fragmentation of power. *The Emperor* and the *Queen of Wands* personify opposing aspects (masculine and feminine) of fire energy which are brought together through (among other things) the image of the *Four of Wands*.
Scorpio: death and rebirth; the principle of die and be reborn, as exemplified by the cards *Death* and *Justice*.
Gemini: the state of tension between the magic of love *(The Magician, The Lovers)* on the one hand and the challenges presented by the higher swords cards *(Eight, Nine* and *Ten of Swords)* on the other.

It has often proved useful to lay a spread of these cards (once or at different times) and leave them to 'settle' for a period of time. Meditate over the cards which belong to 'your' sign of the zodiac. Each time you will find them communicating a new message to you.

Date	Sign of the Zodiac	Planet	Major card of the sign
21 March– 20 April	Aries	Mars	IV – The Emperor
21 April– 20 May	Taurus	Venus	V – The Hierophant
21 May– 21 June	Gemini	Mercury	VI – The Lovers
22 June– 22 July	Cancer	Moon	VII – The Chariot
23 July– 22 August	Leo	Sun	VIII – Strength
23 August– 22 September	Virgo	Mercury	IX – The Hermit
23 September– 22 October	Libra	Venus	XI – Justice
23 October– 21 November	Scorpio	Pluto	XIII – Death
22 November– 20 December	Sagittarius	Jupiter	XIV – Temperance
21 December– 19 January	Capricorn	Saturn	XV – The Devil
20 January– 18 February	Aquarius	Uranus	XVII – The Star
19 February– 20 March	Pisces	Neptune	XVIII – The Moon

Associated court card	Associated number cards	Major card of the planet
Queen of Wands	Wands 2–4	XVI – The Tower
King of Pentacles	Pentacles 5–7	III – The Empress
Knight of Swords	Swords 8–10	I – The Magician
Queen of Cups	Cups 2–4	II – The High Priestess
King of Wands	Wands 5–7	XIX – The Sun
Knight of Pentacles	Pentacles 8–10	I – The Magician
Queen of Swords	Swords 2–4	III – The Empress
King of Cups	Cups 5–7	XX – Judgement
Knight of Wands	Wands 8–10	X – The Wheel of Fortune
Queen of Pentacles	Pentacles 2–4	XXI – The World
King of Swords	Swords 5–7	XXII/0 – The Fool
Knight of Cups	Cups 8–10	XII – The Hanged Man